april

WITHOUT A DOUBT

Bringing Faith to Life

Bishop Thomas J. Tobin

EMMAUS
ROAD
PUBLISHING

FOREWORD BY FRANCIS CARDINAL GEORGE, O.M.I.

WITHOUT A DOUBT

Bringing Faith to Life

Bishop Thomas J. Tobin

EMMAUS
ROAD
PUBLISHING

FOREWORD BY FRANCIS CARDINAL GEORGE, O.M.I.

© 2001
Emmaus Road Publishing
All rights reserved.

Library of Congress
Control Number 2001096878

Published by
Emmaus Road Publishing
a division of Catholics United for the Faith
827 North Fourth Street
Steubenville, Ohio 43952
(800) 398-5470

Cover design and layout by
Beth Hart

Published in the United States of America
ISBN 1-931018-11-1

Contents

Acknowledgements

Saint Thomas the Apostle is my patron saint, as well as the patron of this book and these articles. The well-known story of "doubting Thomas" is featured most prominently in the liturgy of the Second Sunday of Easter when we hear the account of his skepticism at first hearing the news of the Resurrection of Christ.

I've felt for a long time that the name "doubting Thomas" is pretty unfair. What if you and I were known publicly for our weaknesses: "greedy John" or "dishonest Mary"? It seems to me that Thomas merely had a healthy skepticism that, in truth, characterized all the apostles. And keep in mind that, after his initial hesitation, Thomas would live and die bearing courageous witness to his unshakeable faith in the Risen Christ. I have already proposed that Saint Thomas the Apostle be forever known as "faithful Thomas."

In the spirit of "faithful Thomas," these articles have been written with the firm conviction that religious faith, despite the occasional lapses of the believer, has to be applied to the circumstances of everyday life to have any real impact. These articles, written originally for the *Catholic Exponent*, the newspaper of the Diocese of Youngstown, are meant to bridge the gap between the teaching of the Church and our lived experience; to offer some very practical observations about the consequences of our Catholic faith in the "real world."

I am grateful to the clergy, religious, and laity of the Youngstown Diocese who have welcomed these articles and encouraged me to persevere in my efforts.

I am grateful to Mr. Denny Finneran, former editor of the *Exponent*, who suggested the very useful title *Without a Doubt*; and to the current editor, Mr. Lou Jacquet, and his fine staff, for providing a regular home for my thoughts.

I owe a profound debt of gratitude to my secretaries, Carmie and Helene, for their dedication and expertise in preparing the articles for publication and gently leading me away from the security of my electric typewriter to the unfamiliar frontier of the word-processing era.

To His Eminence, Francis Cardinal George, I extend my sincere appreciation for the very kind and generous foreword he provided for this book. His words of endorsement lend far more dignity and credibility to my modest enterprise than it would otherwise deserve.

Finally, with love I dedicate this book to my parents, Raymond and Mary, who first taught me the value and joy of living our Catholic faith in the unremarkable circumstances of everyday life.

Mary, Mother of the Church, pray for us.

Most Rev. Thomas J. Tobin
Bishop of Youngstown

Foreword

When a bishop is ordained by Christ in the Catholic Church, he is asked: "Will you preach the Gospel faithfully and unceasingly?" This is the ministry emphasized by the Second Vatican Council's teaching on the Church: "Among the more important duties of the bishop, that of preaching the Gospel has pride of place" (*Lumen Gentium*, no. 25). Pope Paul VI reminded bishops that, in union with the successor of Saint Peter, they "receive through the power of their episcopal ordination the authority to teach the revealed truth in the Church. They are teachers of the faith" (*Evangelii Nuntiandi*, no. 68).

The bishop never teaches as an isolated individual but always within that communion which is "the whole people . . . from the bishops to the last of the faithful," a company which is led by the Holy Spirit, who guarantees the indefectibility of the Church in the truth of the faith. The whole body of the faithful has a supernatural appreciation of the faith (*sensus fidei*) when they manifest a universal consent in matters of faith and morals (*Lumen Gentium*, no. 12). That appreciation of the faith is more than public opinion; it cannot be the outcome of opinion polls or the agenda of some self-appointed group within the Church. It is the Spirit-led understanding of revealed truth by the whole Church.

All members of the Church are to be united with their bishops in a living witness to Jesus Christ. Within the Church, by the will of Christ Himself, His apostles and their successors exercise that foundational ministry that leads and authenticates the *sensus fidei*. Christ, in calling the Twelve from the body of

His disciples, founded the community of faith as a hierarchical communion. Within this organic communion, the college of bishops—with the Bishop of Rome and under him—each bishop exercises his teaching office. It is a measure of the divinely authorized nature of this task that, when the bishops "in matters of faith and morals . . . speak in the name of Christ . . . the faithful are to accept their teaching and adhere to it with religious assent of soul" (*Lumen Gentium*, no. 25).

A faithful bishop cannot be silent. He must speak the truth revealed by God in Jesus Christ (cf. 1 Cor. 9:16). In a world where contradictory voices are loud and sharp, how to speak is a question a bishop asks each day. Within his own diocese, there are so many other expectations of the bishop, so much required in the way of administration, so many demands for help and recognition, that the question is sometimes put off. Yet, if he is not visibly and audibly the teacher he has been equipped by Christ to be, the bishop is failing in his sacred vocation.

These considerations on the office of bishop explain why this collection of homilies, addresses, and newspaper columns by Bishop Thomas Tobin of Youngstown is so heartwarming. In them we catch the voice of the bishop as teacher, we see the pastor feeding the flock, the pastoral leader equipped by the grace of ordination authenticating the *sensus fidei* of his people. As a brother bishop, I thank Bishop Tobin for making available this fruit of the primary task that is his and mine in the Church. His teaching encourages and inspires me in my ministry. I hear in it the voice of the faithful teacher, friendly and openhearted, imbued with the spirit of Catholic ecclesial communion, luminous with the truth Jesus Christ entrusted to His Church.

This book is for a wide variety of readers. Bishop Tobin applies the truths of the faith and the teachings of the Church to everyday life. Without a doubt but with many good questions from daily experience, he bridges the gap between faith and practice. In accessible concepts and language, he helps his readers to grasp what it means to live the faith. I'm grateful to him, as will be all who spend time with this book.

Francis Cardinal George, O.M.I.
Archbishop of Chicago

I

Reflections of a Bishop

"Dear Bishop Tobin"

I f I remember correctly, it was on the old *Perry Como Show* that they sang the jingle, "Letters, we get letters, we get lots and lots of letters." This refrain would introduce a segment of the show in which Perry would sing musical requests sent in by his fans. I think of that jingle occasionally, for in my work I too receive lots and lots of letters. I'd guess that on average I receive about 100 pieces of mail per week. Let me tell you about some of the mail I receive.

Probably half of my mail is throwaway—advertisements for office products and services, books and manuscripts people think I should read, newsletters from organizations I've never heard of, computer-generated appeals addressed to "Mr. and Mrs. Diocese of Youngstown." Disposing of this mail helps to clear my desk in a hurry.

The other half of the mail receives far more serious attention and falls, generally, into a few broad categories: complaints, commendations, invitations, suggestions, and reports.

You're probably not surprised to learn that I sometimes receive letters from unhappy customers! In our radio talk show age, everyone's an expert, and no one hesitates to share his or her opinion. And people do complain—about the laws of the Church and diocesan policies; about pastors and members of parish staffs; about me and things I've written, said, or done. Really, I don't mind getting letters of complaint because most often the letter writers have invested their time and energy and are sincerely concerned about the well-being of the Church.

Letters that are personally insulting to me or to others receive very short shrift, for even complainers are bound by laws of fairness and Christian charity. I always get a kick out of letters that attack aggressively but end on a cheerful Christian note. For example:

> Dear Bishop Tobin—I think that decision you made was the stupidest thing I've ever heard. You're ruining the Church and destroying the diocese. Why don't you go back to Pittsburgh where you belong? Sincerely yours in Christ, Ms. Jane Doe.

Anonymous letters aren't taken very seriously, either, for they are inherently unfair. It's unreasonable for a person to send an unsigned letter, make a serious allegation about someone else, and expect me to do something about it. Anonymous letters are impossible to substantiate or respond to and are discarded without a second thought.

In responding to letters of complaint, I try to follow the principle of subsidiarity. For example, if a person writes to complain about something their pastor said or did, the immediate question is, "Have you discussed this with your pastor?" Within the Church, reconciliation presumes that we have first addressed a problem with the person who offended us before we have recourse to higher authority.

Fortunately, not all the mail I receive is negative, and some letters contain beautiful personal stories or words of encouragement. It always brightens my day to receive a positive letter that praises a decision I've made, a program we've started, or the excellent work of one of our priests, religious, or diocesan staff members. We all need a pat on the back once in a while, and we would do well to say and write encouraging things to one another a little more often.

I receive lots of invitations in the mail to attend parish events, community gatherings, or personal social affairs. Of course it's always flattering to be invited and I do appreciate the thoughtfulness of someone asking me to be with them. One of the more frustrating aspects of my work, however, is that it's simply impossible to attend *everything*.

Parish events take priority for me, for that's where a shepherd should be, in the midst of his flock. Liturgical and devotional activities are particularly important, because it's good that a bishop lead his people in prayer. However, as much as I'd love to attend the wonderful spaghetti, pierogi, or roast beef dinners, and parish festivals and fund-raisers, there just aren't enough days in a week to allow me to do so.

People often write to share ideas about how to improve the life of the Church, and these ideas are welcome. Not that every suggestion is accepted, but I appreciate the fact that people are thinking creatively and taking time to offer their suggestions. Some suggestions, of course, are beyond my authority to do anything about because they involve the laws of God or the Universal Church. I can't change the teaching of the Church about the permanence of marriage, the ordination of women to the priesthood, or the number of sacraments. Other ideas are more helpful and receive serious consideration in the consultative process of the diocese.

My mailbag also includes lots of reports—from the United States Conference of Catholic Bishops, the Catholic Conference of Ohio, ecumenical associations, various boards on which I serve, and from our diocesan offices—reports about finances, schools and religious education programs, Catholic Charities, clergy assignments, religious communities in the diocese, and so forth. Keeping up with the river of information that flows across my desk is a real challenge and allows little additional time for more serious or even recreational reading.

The mail I receive is certainly revealing of the diversity of the Church today. I get letters from cardinals, bishops, priests, deacons, religious, and laity; from school kids and senior citizens; from people within the diocese and around the world; from liberals and conservatives. One day a couple of months ago I received a letter from the pseudo-Catholic, extremely liberal group Call to Action, inviting me to attend their annual meeting. The very next piece of mail I opened was from a group of very conservative Catholics insisting that the Church had drifted into heresy and demanding that we return to the "Faith of Our Fathers," that the Mass be said only and always in Latin. A bishop is sometimes like the rope in a tug-of-war!

A few other random thoughts about the mail I receive . . .

Some people, in an attempt to take a short-cut, I suppose, send mail directly to my home, thinking that there it will receive more personal attention. That's a big mistake. I have no secretarial assistance at home and the mail I receive there is often set aside or entirely disregarded. The best way to receive a response is to send mail to my office where we are equipped to handle it, where it becomes part of a well-established routine. And by the way—I do personally read every piece of mail that is sent to me, even if I should decide to pass it on to someone else for proper disposition.

Occasionally people are dismayed that I don't personally respond to all the mail I receive. Recently one gentleman was outraged that I didn't personally answer his letter, suggesting that if he had been a wealthy Catholic his letter would have received my personal attention. What he didn't understand is that my forwarding his letter to a member of the diocesan staff actually ensured that he would receive a prompt and well-informed response, far more so than if I had responded myself.

I try to keep up with the mail as well as I can, answering at least within a month, usually more quickly. But if the mail arrives at an especially busy season, or at a time when I've been out of the office for a meeting, retreat, or vacation, it might take a little longer to respond.

In short, I "get letters, lots and lots of letters," and the mail becomes a significant part of my ministry. But that's a good sign, I think, a sign that the Church is alive and well, that our people really do care and want to be involved. So, keep those cards and letters coming. I'll be worried if they ever stop!

Golf Lessons

"Hey, Bishop Tobin, that'd be a great score on a golf course," said the young man of junior-high age. The only problem was that we were in a bowling alley at the time!

The sad truth is that both my bowling and my golf scores hover dangerously around 100, usually falling on the wrong side of my personal Mendoza line. But each spring as the weather improves, I'm ready to put away my bowling shoes and, once again, take my athletic prowess out-of-doors and onto the golf course.

Time doesn't permit me to play much golf anymore, but I enjoy it and find it relaxing. Golf for me, and most golfers I think, is more than a game. Golf is a paradigm of life itself, a fierce test of virtue, a cosmic struggle between right and wrong, good and evil, light and darkness, life and death! (Okay, I'm getting a little too dramatic!) Golf does, however, teach us some very practical lessons.

I recently read a book entitled *Golf in the Kingdom,* written by Michael Murphy. The book is described as "a masterpiece on the mysticism of golf," and the author describes the unique challenge of the game:

> I need not catalogue the game's complexity to make my point: you know all about the long and short shots; all the nuance of weather, air and grass; all the emotion and vast resolution; all the schemes for success and delusions of grandeur, and the tall tales unnumbered; the trials of patience and fiendish frustrations; all the suicidal thoughts and glimpses of the millennium. We all have a golfing friend we have had to nurse past a possible breakdown or listen to

patiently while he expounded his latest theory of the game. How often have we seen a round go from an episode of the Three Stooges to the agonies of King Lear—perhaps in the space of one hole! I will never forget a friend who declared after his tee shot that he wanted to kill himself, but when the hole was finished said with total sincerity that he had never been so happy in his entire life!

Now I can't begin to compete with the profound insights of *Golf in the Kingdom*, but I would like to offer my own version of some of life's lessons learned the hard way, on the golf course:

Golf insists on the fundamental equality of all people. The moment you step onto the first tee, social and economic distinctions cease, and all people are equal in the sight of the golf gods. The only thing that matters from that point on is how you hit the ball. On the golf course it doesn't matter if you're rich or poor, Democrat or Republican, liberal or conservative, management or labor, religious or lay, deacon, priest, or bishop. I've yet to see a crozier and miter on a golf course. The game of golf is a great equalizer, stripping away all the layers we've superimposed over God's original design.

The only exception to this rule of equality is the chivalrous practice of providing a special tee for "the ladies." If the Equal Rights Amendment is ever passed, I hope it's applied first of all on the golf course! However, I'm told that some courses now offer special gold tees for senior citizens, an advantage I might use in the near future.

Golf is an excellent teacher of patience. No game in the universe is more frustrating than golf. One day you play like a PGA pro, and the next like you've never held a club before. One hole can be a masterpiece, the next an unmitigated disaster. One shot slices wildly to the right, the next a pull hook to the left. And who knows why? Remember, there are no adversaries in golf, no one trying to stop your ball, defend the green, or knock you on your backside as you swing. Every mistake you make is yours, and yours alone!

Golf reminds us that in life, too, we need a good dose of patience. Sometimes things just don't go our way or turn out the way we had hoped. Sometimes we don't know why; sometimes there's just no discernible reason. How often we need to be patient with ourselves, with others, and even with God.

Golf teaches how beneficial it is to stay on the straight and narrow. The surest way to get in trouble on the golf course is to hit the ball off the fairway. Drive the ball to the right or left and you're in the rough, in the water or the woods, none of which is good. The best way to score well is to hit the ball far and straight.

Isn't life like that, too? Live in a way that is morally straight and upright, keep the commandments, follow God's law, and you'll never get into much trouble. But, play around, break the rules, try to cheat, and inevitably you'll pay the price and end up way out-of-bounds. So many problems of life are caused by leaving the moral fairway God has mapped out for us.

Golf forces us to confront our fears and overcome them. Nothing causes me more fear than having to hit the ball over water. And it's all psychological. I might be playing the game of my life, hitting the ball really well—until water appears on the course. And you know what happens then—sweaty palms, dry throat, nervous tremors, and chunk, a ball in the water! The only way to deal with water is to recognize it's there, enjoy the challenge, relax, and play your game!

What are the fears and anxieties of your life? Are they able to be changed, or are they beyond your control? In any event, you need first to recognize the hazard, accept the challenge, and play your game. Don't be paralyzed by the fears and anxieties that come your way.

From golf we learn the importance of the little things of life. Golf is a game of precision. Hit the ball 300 yards, but land in a tiny divot, and you've got a problem. Turn your grip on the club just a fraction, and a perfect drive is pushed far into the deep, dark forest. Miss a speed putt by just an inch and watch helplessly as it rolls off the green, turning a possible birdie into a sure bogey.

Little things are also important in the game of life. A few extra minutes of study each day turn a "C" into an "A." A simple word of encouragement or gratitude can make a friend for life. One good deed can brighten a day and renew a soul. Never discount the value of the little things in life.

Golf teaches us to keep perspective. Golf is supposed to be fun and relaxing, but lots of people take it way too seriously. I've played with people who get angry and frustrated, curse and swear, and throw their clubs. That's no fun. I've known people who got so frustrated with the game that they gave it up completely!

We need to keep a balanced perspective on life. There are so many angry people in the world today. How often we lose control of our emotions because of the minor difficulties and inconveniences we encounter in daily life. The little problems become way too important and rob us of our peace and happiness. For heaven's sake, literally, keep some perspective. Relax and have fun.

Golf teaches us to live in hope and look to the future with confidence. I've never had a hole in one; never even close. A green-in-one is cause for celebration for me! But I'll keep trying. Someday, maybe, through sheer luck and divine intervention, I'll get my ace.

Hope is the virtue that points to the future. Perhaps you're nurturing a dream that seems far off and unattainable. Don't give up. Keep trying. Live in hope. Through your perseverance and with God's help, perhaps you'll attain that dream, maybe you'll reach that unreachable star—and probably a long time before I get my hole in one.

So there you have it . . . my personal reflections on the lessons of golf.

Be assured, I won't give up my day job to join the PGA Tour, or now, lamentably, the Senior PGA Tour. I've accepted the fact that I'll never be another Arnold Palmer, Jack Nicklaus, or Tiger Woods.

But I'll keep playing golf, whenever I can. Because it's fun. And because I learn so much.

Celibate on Valentine's Day

Ah, Valentine's Day! Dining and dancing, romance and roses, and . . . celibacy!

In our society, celibacy is always counter-cultural, but never more so than on Valentine's Day, our annual festival of human love and affection. Valentine's Day is for a celibate what an ice storm is for a road crew, a time of particular challenge and peril. It's in this context that I've chosen to write on the challenges of celibacy and its value for the Church and the world.

One of the problems priests face today is that they're expected to be simultaneously celibate and intimate. The Church, at least in the Latin Rite, requires its priests to be celibate, to forego the pleasures of marriage, family, and romantic involvement. At the same time, the Church and the world expect priests to be "intimate," to be men who are warm, loving, caring, and compassionate; men who relate well to young and old, male and female.

That's the dilemma—priests are expected to get close to their flock, but not "too close"; to be deeply involved in the lives of people without becoming involved "with" them; to safeguard the discipline of celibacy without becoming what one author calls "consecrated refrigerators."

The question can be framed in two ways, I suppose. How can I value and foster a commitment to celibacy in the midst of a very intimate world? Or, how can I be an authentically intimate person and still remain faithful to the rigors of celibacy?

First, we need to affirm in the clearest of terms that celibacy is a beautiful gift a man freely offers in response to the Lord's invitation to serve in the priesthood. It is, or should be, a joyful and fulfilling donation of self.

A problem arises, however, when we describe celibacy in negative terms, by what it's not: no marriage, no children, no romantic attachments. No wonder celibacy becomes so burdensome. It's rather depressing, isn't it, to define a major part of one's existence by focusing on what we can't do?!

I recall a powerful scene from the popular movie *The Thornbirds*, in which Father Ralph, already enamored of his beautiful young friend, Meggie, struggles to get out of his priestly vestments, including his cincture, following Mass. As he wrestles with the entangled cincture, he cries out in a moment of anger and confusion, "God, get me out of this!" He speaks not only of his cincture, but of the celibacy that restricts him from pursuing his love for Meggie.

I know priests who have experienced the same conflict, even if they haven't expressed it in such dramatic terms. And without a doubt, celibacy can be a difficult, lonely, painful road.

But in fact, celibacy is not intended to be a destructive experience, but a positive and life-giving way of relating to Christ and His people. It does, of course, limit the nature and extent of relationships with others, but then again, so does marriage.

In one of the rectories I lived as a parish priest, the dear, gentle lady who was our housekeeper said to us on more than one occasion: "There's a reason you guys aren't married; probably can't find any woman who would put up with you!" I like to believe that's not completely true, but in any case, the reasons for celibacy are much deeper than that!

In *Pastores Dabo Vobis*, a 1992 Apostolic Exhortation on the Formation of Priests, Pope John Paul II writes:

> The synod fathers clearly and forcefully expressed their thought on this matter in an important proposal which deserves to be quoted here . . . : "While in no way interfering with the discipline of the Oriental churches, the synod [on the

formation of priests], in the conviction that perfect chastity in priestly celibacy is a charism, reminds priests that celibacy is a priceless gift of God for the Church and has a prophetic value for the world today" (no. 29).

The document goes on to list and explain the positive motives for celibacy in the priesthood. It is an expression of the desire for total union with Christ. It is a manifestation of the priest's undivided commitment to the service of God's people. It is a compelling and effective sign of the kingdom of God, a kingdom with values different from those of the world.

But what of the other side of the coin, the intimacy which allows a priest to become a wholesome and healthy person? It's important to emphasize that intimacy here does not refer to romantic involvement or genital sexuality. It connotes, rather, relationships that are open, honest, personal, and mature. A Capuchin priest, Father Keith Clarke, describes intimacy as "the human experience of being mutually 'transparent' in a way that two personalities are joined." Another author refers to intimacy as "those strengths which enable a person to share deeply with another."

The ability to be an "intimate person" is essential to the full development of a priest as a person, a minister, and a disciple of Christ. *Pastores Dabo Vobis* itself speaks of the need for a priest to have an affective personality:

> Of special importance is the capacity to relate to others. This is truly fundamental for a person who is called to be responsible for a community and to be a "man of communion." This demands that the priest not be arrogant, or quarrelsome, but affable, hospitable, sincere in his words and heart, prudent and discreet, generous and ready to serve, capable of opening himself to clear and brotherly relationships and of encouraging the same in others. . . . Affective maturity presupposes an awareness that love has a central role in human life. . . . Man cannot live without love (nos. 43-44).

Is it possible to be both celibate and intimate? Sure it is. It's a real challenge, of course, and while most are successful, a few fall short of the goal. We need to be understanding and forgiving when they do. The joy and personal fulfillment that the combination of celibacy and intimacy produces, however, is incomparable.

For priests (and religious) the ultimate reason for celibacy and the true object of intimacy is the Lord Jesus Christ. This is the same Jesus who lived a solitary life for the sake of the kingdom, the Jesus who shared loving and personal thoughts with His disciples the night before He died, the Jesus who called His disciples "friends" and gave them the most intimate gifts, His own Body and Blood.

To succeed in being both celibate and intimate, a priest needs a consistent and personal commitment to prayer, and prayer before the Blessed Sacrament is especially fruitful in this regard. It is here that an intimate friendship with Jesus is nourished, that we find the discernment, balance, and integration required to be simultaneously celibate and intimate.

It is important, it seems to me, that members of the Church clearly understand the nature of priestly celibacy, that they appreciate the depth of the sacrifice a priest has made, and that they support that commitment. The faithful should offer sincere friendship to their priests, but in a way that respects their need for appropriate "distance." After all, priests are men consecrated to the Lord, men "set apart" not from others, but for others.

Me and My Accordion

This chapter is about the holiday season and family life, but first I want to tell you about me and my accordion.

As a child I took accordion lessons. That's right, for three long years, from fifth grade to eighth. Every Tuesday night my accordion teacher would come to our home for an hour to teach me the basics of the accordion and introduce me to a variety of tunes. (The first song I remember learning was "Pop Goes the Weasel." "Lady of Spain" came much later.)

Actually, I really enjoyed playing the accordion. In the summertime I would open the windows so that the whole neighborhood could enjoy it too. Other kids growing up in Pittsburgh in the 1950s had Roberto Clemente and Bill Mazeroski as heroes; I had Lawrence Welk.

I wasn't a very good accordionist, however. In fact, I was pretty bad. So bad that my first accordion teacher, a young guy named Jim, got really frustrated one Tuesday night, left our house, disappeared, and was never heard from again. I was so bad that the novel *Accordion Crimes* was written about me. My second accordion teacher, Johnny, was a gentle and patient man who stayed with me three years, bravely enduring his penance, richly meriting the eternal reward he now enjoys.

Now, playing the accordion gave rise to one of the most important and endearing of Tobin family traditions. On each of the major holidays—Thanksgiving, Christmas, and New Year's Day—after a really full dinner, the entire family would retire to the family room to relax, and someone, usually my mom or dad, anxious to hear the fruit of the $3-per-hour lessons, would coax me to play the accordion.

After just the second or third song, the following would occur: Inky my dog would begin to howl; my brothers and sister would complain and leave the house; and mom and dad would initiate a polite conversation with our guests. ("It could have been worse; he could have taken drum lessons.") Within minutes the television was on again, and I was told that if I insisted on playing the accordion, I should go to my room, close the door, and play as quietly as possible. Thus humiliated, my holidays often ended in sadness.

I don't play the accordion much anymore.

The holiday season is surely a time to celebrate your family life and rekindle the traditions that are part of your story. Perhaps the traditions of your family are religious or cultural—attendance at Midnight Mass or special ethnic foods; perhaps more personal and intimate—a special remembrance of a deceased family member; or perhaps just silly—Grandpap always falling asleep in his favorite chair or Uncle Joe telling the same story over and over again. Holiday traditions are important for families. They reveal the joy of family life and simultaneously enrich it.

The Church has a beautiful message about family life:

> "The Christian family constitutes a specific revelation and realization of ecclesial communion, and for this reason it can and should be called a *domestic church*." It is a community of faith, hope, and charity. . . . The Christian family is a communion of persons, a sign and image of the communion of the Father and the Son in the Holy Spirit (Catechism, nos. 2204-05, original emphasis, footnote omitted).

These are certainly challenging and lofty words, and sometimes the reality of family life seems so different. Does your family always reflect the perfect unity of the Holy Trinity? Probably not. Family life is not always serene. It encounters real obstacles in the world today. Our society, especially the popular media, does little to support authentic family values. There are immense financial pressures on families. The pace of society is such that it is nearly impossible for families to spend much time together: Parents, sometimes both of them, work long hours, and even the children are trapped in a rat race of sporting events and social activities. The kids are worn out by the time they're teenagers.

That's why it's so helpful to reflect upon the Holy Family—Jesus, Mary, and Joseph—whose story is the centerpiece of the holiday season. In doing so, however, we shouldn't idealize them, reducing them to the blissful images found on Christmas cards. The Holy Family was very real and faced incredible challenges.

Jesus, Mary, and Joseph weren't always happy. Recall that Jesus was born in the most difficult and dangerous of circumstances. The Holy Family had to flee their homeland to protect the life of their child. Tradition tells us that Joseph died early and that Mary was a single parent raising Jesus by herself. As Jesus grew older He was the itinerant preacher who had "nowhere to lay His head." He was ridiculed by many, His message often rejected. And Mary, His Mother, could only watch in silence as her beloved Son was unjustly condemned, suffered great torment, and died the death of a common criminal on a cross.

Whatever the experience of your family, you can learn a great deal from the experience of the Holy Family.

We learn, for example, the importance of *faith*. Mary and Joseph were people of deep faith. Even before the birth of Jesus, God was the center of their lives. They were raised in devout Jewish families and had an ongoing friendship with the Lord. They were completely open to God's voice and were anxious to do whatever God asked of them.

Faith is essential for your family, too. Without faith, your life is incomplete and shallow. Your religious faith is the glue that keeps your family together, especially during difficult times. It is the virtue that imparts meaning to your life, giving you motivation for doing good. Faith provides direction, support, and comfort in all that you encounter.

We see also the wonderful *generosity* of the Holy Family. Jesus, Mary, and Joseph were generous in responding to their Heavenly Father and in relating to one another. They were always able to move beyond their own selfish needs and desires to be keenly aware of God's place in their lives and sensitive to the real and practical needs of one another.

Generosity is absolutely one of the keys to a successful family life today, and it manifests itself in many ways. All family members have to make a conscious decision to place the needs of others ahead of their own: spouses to each other, parents to children, children to parents, and brothers and sisters to one another. And the whole family should seek to be generous in relating to its neighbors, the Church, and the world.

The holidays bring out the best, and sometimes the worst, of family life. But I hope that in the next holiday season you'll make a special effort to love your family. It's not always easy, and it's never perfect. But it is God's plan for us and the setting from which we can best move toward eternal life.

Now if you're lucky, there's no one in your family who plays the accordion, but if there is, be nice! And be attentive to your own family traditions: cherish them, practice them, and pass them on to your children.

Building Bridges

When the Fifth Avenue bridge reopened, it was great news for the residents of Youngstown.

Bridges are important. They cross over impassable and sometimes dangerous terrain and allow us to travel from one location to another. Without bridges our travel is limited and we live in isolation and solitude.

On a human level we need to build bridges as well, bridges with other people. We do so in our activities, our relationships, and especially in the way we speak to one another. Our proper use of language, with one another and about one another, is essential to the building of good communities and long-term, productive relationships.

Our speech should always be honest, civil, patient, and charitable. This is especially true when we disagree with one another and our bonds are tested. That's how we build bridges. When we resort to judgments, public accusations, and private gossip, bridges are destroyed and walls are erected.

This is an important rule, first of all in our families. Husbands and wives, parents and children, brothers and sisters must speak words of love if those family ties are to be strong and supportive.

A husband leaves his clothes piled in a corner on the floor and his wife is upset. "You're a slob," she says. "You're a nag," he replies. Parents constantly criticize their teenage children, damaging any sense of self-respect at a time it is most needed. Teenagers talk back to their parents with complete disregard for the Fourth Commandment. Brothers and sisters bicker constantly about the smallest of affairs, making it impossible to have even one peaceful meal. Because of the tensions of everyday life, families have to work especially hard to speak to one another in love.

In our society it is important to use proper speech as well, for the sake of the common good, the sake of progress. How often the opposite prevails. Public officials point fingers at one another and the average citizen suffers from the political gridlock. Political campaigns become increasingly personal and negative, the voter is turned off, and public issues are never properly addressed. Are political campaigns and the politicians who wage them exempt from the law of love?

In the Church, too, and perhaps especially in the Church, we use language to build bridges to one another. The Church is, after all, the Body of Christ, and charity is the premise of our relationships.

When members of parish societies compete for the limited space and resources of their parish, they need to avoid unkind words and angry exchanges. When people become irritated with their pastor, they need to speak honestly, of course, but respectfully and charitably as well. How often, though, we hear of disgruntled parishioners attaching labels to their priests, causing dissension in the parish family, withdrawing support, and staying away from the sacraments, harming only themselves and their families.

Sometimes people will disagree with their bishop. That's understandable, for bishops, too, are very human. Members of the Church are free, of course, to have opinions that vary from those of their bishops, unless the question involves a matter of faith and morals. Then it's no longer just an opinion of the bishop, but a teaching of the Church.

But even when we disagree with a bishop, the language needs to be respectful and charitable. Otherwise, it's impossible to maintain respect for legitimate authority and love for the Church.

Once I heard about a bishop in another part of the country who made a decision that upset some of his flock. One of the "faithful" wrote to that bishop saying that she wished that the bishop's mother had had an abortion so that he would have never been born. And this from someone who claimed to be a lifetime Catholic and follower of Jesus.

Our Holy Father, even in addressing the most difficult and challenging of issues, speaks always with respect, concern, and love for others, even those he knows will disagree with him. His critics, however, are often far less kind. They tear up his picture on stage, ridicule him in newspaper cartoons, and say vile things about the Vicar of Christ—this Pope who is such a good and holy and gentle man.

We long for affirmation and support from those in authority. But it is a two-way street, isn't it? And nothing is more revealing about our inner self and our attitude toward others than our use of language.

The Gospel tells us that whatever we do to the least of our brothers and sisters we do to Jesus. This is true also for our speech. Whatever we say to and about others, we say to and about Christ Himself.

Let's step back and examine our conscience about the way we speak—in our families, our community, our Church. Are we fair? Are we patient? Are we charitable? Do we build bridges or tear them down?

Questions of the Bible

So often we look to the Bible for answers—answers to questions of faith, answers to life's most perplexing dilemmas. And that's the way it should be. After all, as Saint Paul wrote, "All Scripture is inspired by God and profitable for teaching, for reproof, for correction, and for training in righteousness" (2 Tim. 3:16).

But we should also pay close attention to the questions of the Bible. The Bible has many questions that lead to the revelation of great and lasting truths. Consider the following:

"Where are you?" (Gen. 3:9). God asks Adam this question very early in the Bible. Adam answers, "I heard the sound of thee in the garden, and I was afraid, because I was naked" (Gen. 3:10). This newfound fear, the need to hide from God, was a terrible consequence of sin.

We were created to live in harmony with God and one another. But sin alienates us from God and others. Because of sin we find ourselves hiding from God, fearful of His just anger and punishment. Even at the moment of the very first sin, however, God immediately begins to implement His plan for salvation. We can try to hide from God, but He always finds us.

"Where is the lamb?" (Gen. 22:7). This seemingly innocuous question is filled with suspense. It is the question of Isaac to Abraham as they prepare the sacrifice for the Lord. The answer, as God tests the faith of Abraham, is that Isaac himself was to be the sacrificial lamb offered to the Lord.

This question serves as a remote preparation for the Messiah. The question, "Where is the lamb?" would cascade down through the centuries and through generations of the Chosen People until John the Baptist recognized Jesus, pointed to Him, and said, "Behold, the Lamb of God!" At every Eucharist the priest again answers Isaac's question by presenting the Eucharist and declaring, "This is the Lamb of God."

"Who am I?" (Ex. 3:11). From the midst of the burning bush God tells Moses that He has witnessed the affliction of His people, heard their cry of complaint, and chosen Moses to lead them out of slavery. Moses is astounded by this divine commission and contends that he is unable to do what God has asked. God never directly answers Moses' question, never affirms Moses' personal qualifications, but responds simply, "I will be with you."

The example of Moses is very helpful for us, especially as we make decisions about our vocation in life. God never presumes to depend on our human ability to accomplish His purposes, but leads us only to trust in His power. "I will be with you," He promises.

"How can this be?" (Lk. 1:34). The New Testament, too, is filled with significant questions. This is the question Mary poses to the angel upon learning that she has been chosen to be the Mother of God. Affirming her virginity, Mary doesn't understand how she could become a mother. But in the response of the angel, "The Holy Spirit will come upon you," Mary discerns God's favor in her life and submits to His will.

Mary's unshakable faith, her predisposition to God, enabled her to recognize God's action in her life and allowed her to overcome very understandable fears and anxieties. And for us as well, authentic faith should be a constant companion, helpful not only in times of crisis, but always.

"And who is my neighbor?" (Lk. 10:29). Jesus was often involved with questions and answers. This is the question of the lawyer who wished to justify himself before Jesus. In response to this challenge, Jesus tells the beautiful story of the

Good Samaritan, indicating that the true neighbor was the stranger, the foreigner.

With His answer, Jesus emphasizes that charity knows no boundaries, that being a good neighbor is not limited by race, religion, or nationality. This lesson is important to remember whenever we hear the slogan "charity begins at home." In fact, that's just the opposite of what Jesus taught.

"Teacher, what good deed must I do, to have eternal life?" (Mt. 19:16). The rich young man approaches Jesus seeking holiness and personal fulfillment. Jesus instructs him to keep the commandments of the Lord. The man responds that he has always done so, but still feels empty. Jesus gently leads the young man one step further and says, "If you would be perfect, go sell what you possess and give to the poor . . . and come, follow me" (Mt. 19:21). The young man went away sad, for his possessions were many.

One can only speculate about the young man's life after that. He probably remained virtuous and prosperous, but unfulfilled. He is the archetype of many people in our society who are rich in material possessions, but spiritually impoverished. The following of Jesus always requires an emptying of self, a personal sacrifice. There is no other way!

"But who do you say I am?" (Mt. 16:15). The disciples have just told Jesus what people think of Him—that He is John the Baptist, Elijah, or one of the prophets. Jesus insists on knowing what they, His closest followers, believe about Him. In response, Peter professes his faith: "You are the Christ, the Son of the living God" (Mt. 16:16). Peter and the other apostles would spend the remainder of their lives answering this question, not only with convincing words, but with heroic deeds.

Now—who do you say Jesus is? And does the answer to that question make any discernible difference in your life? Think about it! As the apostles discovered, believing in Jesus demands much more than a few easy words.

"**What have you done?**" (Jn. 18:35). That's the question Pontius Pilate poses to Jesus. This dialogue leads Jesus to explain the true nature of His kingdom: "My kingship is not of this world" (Jn. 18:36). Pilate, like many others who heard Jesus, never really understood the nature of Jesus' kingdom, the divine purpose of His mission on earth.

Jesus established "an eternal and universal kingdom 'of truth and life, a kingdom of holiness and grace, a kingdom of justice, love, and peace'" (*Gaudium et Spes*, no. 39). Each day we pray, "Thy kingdom come!"

"**Why do you seek the living among the dead?**" (Lk. 24:5). This is the question of the angels to the disciples who went to the tomb to anoint the body of Jesus. They were astonished by what they found, or rather, by what they did not find. They did not find the body of Jesus. He had been raised from the dead!

Our Christian faith, as complicated as it seems sometimes, comes down to this belief, the Resurrection of Christ. Saint Paul teaches that "if Christ has not been raised, then . . . your faith is in vain" (1 Cor. 15:14). No title of Jesus is more revealing than this: "The Living One."

"**Do you love me?**" (Jn. 21:16). Another encounter between Jesus and Peter, another dialogue. This time the Risen Christ challenges Peter to publicly profess his love. Three times Peter would affirm his love for the Lord, a response to the three times he had denied Him just a few days earlier. Perhaps it wasn't so much that Jesus needed to hear of Peter's love; perhaps it was very important for Peter to speak it.

Even Peter's colossal failure didn't cause him to despair. He persevered until he found another opportunity to begin again, to proclaim his love for Jesus. There's an important lesson here. We should never, ever, be discouraged by our human weakness, our failures of faith and love. Every day Jesus asks us, "Do you love me?" and every day we have a new opportunity to say, "Yes, Lord, you know that I love you."

Reflections from Rome

During my journey to Rome for the Jubilee Year pilgrimage, I was reminded once again how much we depend on other people for our safety and comfort whenever we travel, especially when we travel by air. It's not an overstatement to say that our very lives depend on the competence and commitment of others—mechanics, pilots, and navigators, air traffic controllers, and those whose task it is to ensure our security. Our comfort and convenience also depend on other people—those who check us in at the airport, those who schedule and/or cancel flights, the flight attendants who serve us and review our safety, those who handle our baggage at departure and arrival, and of course, our fellow passengers. Whenever we travel, especially when we fly, we really do rely on the kindness of strangers.

Life is like that, too, isn't it? Every day we depend on other people for our safety, security, and health, and our material and spiritual well-being. And other people depend on us! How important it is to be responsible in doing our work, to be open and honest in relating to others.

The second thing that occurred to me during this trip is how well connected people remain today, even when traveling all over the globe. Modern technology makes that possible. In airports in Pittsburgh, Philadelphia, Frankfurt, and Rome, I saw people using laptop computers, cell phones, and pagers to stay in touch. From my hotel room in Rome I was able, through the European version of CNN, to watch the presidential election returns as they were being reported thousands of miles away. (In heading to Rome, I felt a little sorry that the election would be over and done with before I returned home. Little did I know . . .) The Italians and Germans paid close attention to our election, doing their very best to decipher the intricacies of third parties, the popular vote, and the electoral college.

Indeed, we have become a global village with the ability to communicate more easily than ever. I'm reminded, however, that our technical ability has to be accompanied by personal growth. Being hooked up electronically does nothing to ensure a growth in virtue and vision that benefits the common good of our human family.

Traveling certainly requires patience. Because the situation is often beyond our control, we frequently find ourselves needing to wait—for delayed planes, canceled flights, lost baggage, slow companions, and service in hotels and restaurants. But patience is in short supply today. People are often in a hurry and get really upset over the tiniest of problems and disappointments. The recent rise in "road rage" and now "air rage" among airline customers attests to this problem.

Patience is an essential ingredient of a peaceful and productive life. Things don't always go our way. We frequently need to be patient with ourselves, whenever we fall short of the goal; with other people whenever they disappoint us, as they inevitably will; and even with God, whose plans are often different from our own. The path to patience demands that we keep things in perspective, sorting out those events that are temporary annoyances from those that have lasting meaning for us and our loved ones.

The mix of various languages we encounter when traveling abroad teaches us a valuable lesson, too. On a few occasions I used my fractured Italian to converse with others. (In responding to the question of the taxi driver, I answered, "Lufthansa," and then quickly realized he had asked me where I was born!) On other occasions I spoke English without the other party understanding. Sometimes I watched as other pilgrims tried to make themselves understood by those who didn't speak their language. An interesting phenomenon: When people don't speak the same language they tend to speak more loudly to make themselves understood, as if increasing the volume will help someone understand a language they don't speak at all.

Isn't that true also in our public discourse in society and the Church? When disagreements occur we tend to shout at one another, thinking that raising our voice will compel someone else to understand and accept our point of view. Normally, of course, the opposite is true. In our public conversations, when people refrain from rhetoric, avoid personal attacks, and turn down the volume, real understanding grows and solid common ground is discovered.

Spending some time in Rome, I was reminded of the simple faith of the common Roman people. One morning I paid a visit to the neighborhood church close to our hotel, the church called Santa Maria delle Fornaci. I visited there to pray, say the Rosary, and prepare my homily for later in the day. I arrived at the conclusion of the daily Mass, attended by about twenty of the faithful. Then I watched as people filed in to participate in a funeral. For these good people Rome is home, not a tourist site. They relate to Rome not so much as the Eternal City, but rather simply as the place in which they live today and tomorrow.

In that simple church I thought of the strong faith of common people everywhere. We need to be more aware and grateful for the faithful witness of thousands of people in our parishes who often remain behind the scenes, but yet make an immense contribution to the spiritual well-being of the Church. This silent majority of Catholics live in faith, do their best to inspire their children and their grandchildren, and through their generosity provide the foundation of all the ministries, programs, and services of parishes and dioceses throughout the world.

Visiting Rome, I thought of the universal nature of the Catholic Church. Particularly at St. Peter's Square and in St. Peter's Basilica, during Mass and the papal audience, we found ourselves mixing with people from all over the world. Within just a few minutes I heard a variety of languages: English, Italian, French, German, Spanish, Polish, Japanese, Vietnamese, and several others I couldn't begin to identify.

How isolated we can become, particularly as American Catholics. How easily we fall prey to a kind of religious imperialism, thinking our problems are the most important problems, our ways, the only ways. In Rome we see the pope serve as the Chief Shepherd, the Universal Pastor of the entire Catholic Church. Only he could attract so many pilgrims from every corner of the earth, week after week, year after year. What an enormous responsibility he has. How many burdens he bears. How he deserves our appreciation, respect, support, and love.

Finally, the highlight of the trip for me was celebrating the Jubilee liturgy at St. Peter's Basilica and leading several thousand pilgrims, including the 160 from Youngstown, through the holy door, up the main aisle of the basilica to the Altar of the Chair for the Holy Mass. I was surprised to learn, just a half hour before Mass, that I was obliged to say Mass in Latin, something I had never done before, again in deference to the many diverse language groups that would participate in the liturgy.

In processing through the holy door, I understood once again the serious responsibility of being a bishop, of being a shepherd of God's holy people. In that precious moment I carried with me all the members of our diocesan Church—priests, deacons, religious, and laity. As I prayed, I presented our needs, intentions, and prayers to Jesus Christ, the Lord of all history. And I realized, perhaps as never before, what a great privilege and joy it is to be a bishop.

II

'Tis the Season

Advent: To Dispel the Fear

When, on October 22, 1978, I said the words, "Be not afraid!"
in St. Peter's Square, I could not fully know how far they would
take me and the entire Church. . . . Why should we have no fear?
Because man has been redeemed by God. . . . Peoples and nations
of the entire world need to hear these words. Their conscience
needs to grow in the certainty that Someone exists who holds in
His hands the destiny of the passing world.

—Pope John Paul II
Crossing the Threshold of Hope

Some have called it the "zero factor," which means that the
more zeros included in a new year, the more uncertainty and
anxiety will occur as that year approaches. For example, some
people get apprehensive at the beginning of a new decade,
with only one zero, wondering what the next 10 years will
hold. The beginning of a new century, with a double zero,
sees a marked increase of fearful forecasts. And the beginning
of a new millennium, that's the granddaddy of them all, with
dire predictions of natural disasters, political strife, the end
of the world, and the final coming of Christ. The end of our
particular millennium was further traumatized by the Y2K
crisis—the fear that computers would fail, causing the civilized
world to come to a screeching halt!

A late 1999 article from Catholic News Service documented
the extent of the problem:

If you have Internet access, enter the search term "end times"
on your browser. You now have access to at least 22,000
websites eager to enlighten you about what the upcoming
turn of the millennium is all about. How about "The End

Times Blood Bath" or "666 Is Coming" or "Apocalypse Soon"? The basic premise is nothing new. They say the world will end or at least experience some kind of radical or apocalyptic change at the turn of the millennium.

How far removed is this fear-filled future from the hopeful vision held out by the Church and proclaimed so insistently by our Holy Father, Pope John Paul! From the very beginning of his pontificate, the pope has been leading us to joyfully welcome the dawn of a new millennium, calling us to dispel fear and embrace hope. "Be not afraid" were among his first words after being chosen successor of Peter. This hope of ours, he says, is based not on some detached, unrealistic, rose-colored view of the world, but rather on the firm foundation of the goodness of God who created us and Jesus Christ who redeemed us. He bids us to grow in the certainty that "Someone exists who holds in His hands the destiny of the passing world."

Nevertheless, we realize that fear remains a reality. It doesn't go away simply by saying it should. It's part of the human experience. What, then, are the fears in your life? Perhaps you are fearful of economic uncertainty, unemployment, or the loss of your life's savings. Maybe you fear for the future of your children, worrying about their safety, wondering what kind of a world they'll grow up in. Maybe you share the fear of many people about natural disasters, social upheaval, or the declining state of morality. Or perhaps your fears are more personal—you're afraid of growing old, becoming ill, losing independence, and encountering the prospect of death.

Whatever your fears, it's important that you recognize them, name them, grapple with them, and dispel them, especially so that you can pass through the doors of the new millennium unshackled, free, fully able to embrace the promise and hope of the future.

If you have identified any unresolved fear or anxiety in your life, Advent is your time, your season. Focusing as it does on the second coming of Christ at the end of time, as well as His first coming in Bethlehem two thousand years ago, the message of Advent is one of renewed hope and universal peace.

> Advent invites us to revisit hope—to be aware that hope is not wishful thinking. When it dawns on us that hope is certainty, not wishfulness, our eagerness to journey into the future will generate joyful expectation we can count on.[1]

The Advent liturgy is filled to the brim with reasons for hope. The prophecies of Isaiah in particular create a beautiful image of a world in which God is present, active, and caring for His people:

> For out of Zion shall go the law, and the word of the LORD from Jerusalem. He shall judge between the nations, and shall decide for many peoples . . . nation shall not lift up sword against nation, neither shall they learn war any more (Is. 2:3-4).

> There shall come forth a shoot from the stump of Jesse, and a branch shall grow out of his roots. . . . The wolf shall dwell with the lamb, and the leopard shall lie down with the kid. . . . They shall not hurt or destroy in all my holy mountain; for the earth shall be full of the knowledge of the LORD as the waters cover the sea (Is. 11:1, 6, 9).

> In that day the deaf shall hear the words of a book, and out of their gloom and darkness the eyes of the blind shall see. The meek shall obtain fresh joy in the LORD, and the poor among men shall exult in the Holy One of Israel (Is. 29:18-19).

---

[1] John J. McIlhon.

In other Advent passages, too, the Word of God describes a future to be welcomed, not feared:

> Take off the garment of your sorrow and affliction, O Jerusalem, and put on for ever the beauty of the glory from God (Bar. 5:1).

> Sing aloud, O daughter of Zion; shout, O Israel! . . . The LORD has taken away the judgments against you, he has cast out your enemies (Zeph. 3:14-15).

> Rejoice in the Lord always; again, I will say, Rejoice. . . . The Lord is at hand. Have no anxiety about anything (Phil. 4:4-6).

How evident it is, then, that the Advent season propels us to the future, calls us to be full of hope, supremely confident of God's goodness and love.

> Advent means future, because there is a promise made just for us. And God fulfills His promises. God makes history and fulfills it beyond our imagining. History is not an end. It will not stay this way: Something always awaits us. Perhaps we expect too little because we come with our limited wishes.[2]

The fact is, we don't know when Christ will come again to bring human history to its completion. But contrary to the doom-and-gloom-sayers who tremble at the thought of the future, we look forward with joy to the coming of Christ. Every Advent is a time to rekindle that positive, joyful spirit. And how much more so now that we've passed through the holy door of the Great Jubilee into the promise of a new millennium!

---

[2] Matthias P. Cremer, S.C.J.

May your next Advent season be for you a time of "unlimited wishes." May it be a time to dispel fear from your life and replace it with hope, founded on a God who "holds in His hands the destiny of the passing world," and on His Son Jesus Christ, who is forever the light of the world.

Spring Training

Throughout the South and Southwest, spring training camps for major league baseball have begun. This is an important time for baseball teams. Players will work hard to get their bodies back in shape after a long and lazy winter; they will practice the basic skills of their sport: hitting, running, fielding, and throwing. They will also seek to improve their teamwork. The discipline of February and March will pay dividends throughout the long season that stretches into August and September and, for the best of teams, October.

Perhaps the most important feature of spring training is its spirit of unbridled confidence and optimism. At this point, every rookie hopes to make the team, and every team sees itself as a champion. Everyone starts with a clean slate, and every team is undefeated.

Christians also have their spring training. It's called the season of Lent. It strikes me that there are many parallels between this spiritual spring training and that of baseball.

In this season we try to get ourselves back into shape spiritually. With prayer, fasting, and good works, we practice the basic skills of the spiritual life. While we try to grow stronger as individual disciples of Christ, we also become more conscious of our team, the Church. We prepare to welcome the rookies, the catechumens, onto the team. A productive Lent serves us well in our Christian lives not only these forty days, but throughout the whole liturgical year.

The most important aspect of Lent is the attitude we carry into it. We need a positive spirit, some sense of enthusiasm. Lent offers a great opportunity for us, a chance to make a new beginning. We eagerly accept the discipline of Lent so that we can share the joy of Easter. But the price of that victory is sacrifice. As the common saying goes, "no pain, no gain!"

The Second Vatican Council spoke clearly about the meaning of Lent:

> The Lenten season has a twofold character: 1) it recalls baptism or prepares for it; 2) it stresses a penitential spirit. By these meanings especially, Lent readies the faithful for celebrating the paschal mystery after a period of closer attention to the Word of God, and more ardent prayer (*Sacrosanctum Concilium*, no. 109).

Another author, Father Brian Moore, S.J., expands on this theme:

> Lent is intelligible only in the light of its climax, Easter. The beginning is in ashes; the end in the paschal fire. The discipline of Lent is not an end in itself but a time of preparation of oneself to enter as fully as possible, in mind and heart, into the paschal mystery of the death and resurrection of Jesus. . . . We bow our heads to receive these cold grey ashes at the beginning of Lent only with a view of warming ourselves at the bright Easter fire at its end.[1]

In other words, the Lenten practices we undertake—daily Mass, Stations of the Cross, acts of charity, "giving up" of desserts, entertainment, or personal convenience—can be useful. But why we do these things is just as important as what we do.

The traditional pillars of the Lenten season—prayer, fasting, and good works—are meant to bring about a change of heart,

---

[1] *The Gospel Day by Day through Lent* (Collegeville, Minn.: Liturgical Press, 1992), 10-11.

a radical transformation of our lives. They should help us become better people and stronger Christians. In short, they help us achieve the goal proclaimed by Saint Paul in the second reading of the Ash Wednesday liturgy: "We beseech you on behalf of Christ, be reconciled to God" (2 Cor. 5:20).

This call to penance is an integral part of our Christian faith and an important tradition of the Catholic Church. The centrality of this issue was highlighted not too long ago when the U.S. bishops discussed the possibility of returning to Friday abstinence throughout the entire year. The reaction to the bishops' proposal was strong and swift. One would think that the bishops had asked every family to sacrifice their firstborn! And there was a lot of misunderstanding about the proposal.

First, the bishops' discussion was just that—simply a discussion about the advisability of renewing the traditional Friday discipline.

Second, recall that the Church never eliminated the fact that Fridays are meant to be days of penance. Canon law reminds us:

> All members of the Christian faithful in their own way are bound to do penance in virtue of divine law. In order that all may be joined in a common observance of penance, penitential days are prescribed. . . . All Fridays through the year and the time of Lent are penitential days and times throughout the universal church (canons 1249-50).

Therefore, if Fridays have lost their penitential character for us, it is by widespread neglect, not by legislation.

Third, the proposal discussed by the bishops would not seek to re-impose the strict observance of Friday abstinence under the pain of sin, as we knew in the past. It would invite members of the Church to voluntary abstinence, fasting, or other acts of self-discipline and penance.

And finally, the bishops suggested that a renewed emphasis of Friday penance could be attached to the intention of promoting respect for human life. Offering prayer, sacrifice, and good works for particular intentions is not at all new to the Church. This proposal would give millions of Catholics a way of participating in the pro-life cause in a spiritual and specific manner. It does not suggest that other pro-life activities, or any other works of the Church, should cease.

As you see, whether we speak about the season of Lent or the regular discipline of Fridays throughout the year, penance is an essential and fruitful part of the Christian life. Spiritual discipline, whatever its form, has several purposes: it strengthens our resolve to overcome sin and grow in virtue; it reminds us to be attentive to the poor who go without, not voluntarily, but because they lack the basic necessities of life; and it relates us to Jesus who Himself fasted and prayed, and who said: "If any man would come after me, let him deny himself and take up his cross daily and follow me" (Lk. 9:23).

Lent is good for us. Yet some resist the invitation. Isn't it ironic that in an age and culture where so much time and money is spent on keeping our bodies strong and beautiful, so many people are reluctant to undertake even simple practices that would help their spiritual lives?

May the season of Lent be for you a truly blessed and fruitful time. May this spiritual spring training lead you to the championship of eternal life!

The Easter Vigil: A Time of Birth

We stand in front of our past
which closes and opens at the same time. . . .
Return to each place where a man has died; return to the place
where he was born. The past is the time of birth, not of death.
—Archbishop Karol Wojtyla, "Easter Vigil 1966"

No ceremony of the liturgical year is more important or dramatic than the Easter Vigil. Filled with sign and symbol, it is the place where death and life converge, a time of new life for the followers of Christ. Stunned into silence by the events of Good Friday, the Church gathers in vigil to await and welcome the Risen Christ. We are enlivened by new members of our community who join our company through Baptism, Confirmation, and the Eucharist. And cleansed by our season of penance, we renew the original grace of Baptism by which we were first joined to Christ our life.

The Easter Vigil, wrapped in mystery and rich in meaning, is the culmination of the Sacred Triduum, the beginning of the Easter Season, and a microcosm of the entire Christian life. The goal of the Vigil is to achieve and celebrate total union with Christ. Each of the symbols of the Easter Vigil has that as its purpose.

The darkness of the Vigil is broken by the lighting and blessing of the new fire and the presentation of the Easter candle, the preeminent symbol of the Risen Christ. As the candle is lighted, the Church prays: "Father, we share in the light of your glory through your Son, the light of the world." And in the solemn preparation of the candle, the priest recalls the centrality of Christ in all history, invoking the dramatic words as he inscribes the candle:

> Christ yesterday and today, the beginning and the end, Alpha, and Omega; all time belongs to him, and all the ages; to him be glory and power, through every age for ever. Amen.

Thus we are reminded of the truth proclaimed once again by the pope in St. Louis in 1999:

> Because Jesus is the Light, we too become light when we proclaim him. . . . [Y]ou believe in the light. . . . You are children of the light! You belong to Christ, and he has called you by name. . . . He came to challenge you to be the light of the world! "The light shines in the darkness and the darkness does not overcome it" (Jn. 1:5).

The next stage of the Easter Vigil is the reading of the Word of God. As many as nine Scripture readings may be used, making this the "mother of all vigils."

The readings recall in summary form the history of salvation. Here we listen to the familiar stories of the creation of the world, the sacrifices of Abraham, the passage through the Red Sea, and the vocation to holiness of the people of Israel. The Letter to the Romans emphasizes the reality of our Baptism by which we are grafted onto Christ. And finally the Gospel, preceded by the joyful and solemn intonation of the Alleluia, proclaims the Good News of the Resurrection of Christ.

Thus in a short span we trace the history of the Word of God from the creation of the world to the glorification of Christ, the Incarnate Word of God. This movement clearly reveals that throughout the history of the world the Word of God has been persistent and efficacious. The Easter Vigil confirms that truth as no other liturgy of the year. The People of God, gathered now in sacred vigil, are not merely passive hearers of the word, but active participants in God's plan of salvation as it continues to unfold in our time.

The Vigil then moves into the liturgy of Baptism, when new members of the Church are initiated through the sacraments. Water becomes the focal point of this part of the rite. As the baptismal water is blessed, the priest prayerfully recalls the many ways God has used water as an instrument of grace. The priest remembers that at the creation of the world, the "Spirit breathed on the waters, making them the wellspring of all holiness." He goes on to recall that the waters of the great flood "made an end of sin and a new beginning of goodness"; that the people of Israel were led out of slavery "through the waters of the Red Sea"; that Jesus was baptized in the waters of the Jordan River; and that water and blood flowed from the side of the crucified Christ, prefiguring the sacramental life of the Church.

All these uses of water in salvation history are fulfilled by the Sacrament of Baptism, that gift of God that washes away original sin, makes us children of God, and opens for us the doors of the Church. In the Easter Vigil liturgy, new members are immersed into the mystery of Christ, and their souls are flooded with His saving grace. In the Easter Vigil liturgy, all members of the Church are sprinkled with water and are invited to renew their Baptism promises and faith commitment to Christ.

Finally, the Easter Vigil reaches its culmination with the celebration of the Eucharist as the gifts of bread and wine become the Body and Blood of the Lord. Through the reception of Holy Communion, we share most fully in the redemption accomplished by Christ in His death and Resurrection. Now, as the Eucharist is consecrated, we move from the realm of pure symbol into a deeper reality. Now the substance of the signs is transformed as they become the reality they signify, the Body and Blood of Christ.

This Eucharist is the Passover of the Lord, the holy banquet Jesus shared at the Last Supper, the sacrifice of Jesus on the Cross, a sharing in the new life of His Resurrection, and the pledge of God's abiding presence with His people on their pilgrim way.

You can see the many ways the ceremonies of the Easter Vigil allow us to experience and express our total union with Christ. On this holy night God is particularly present and active among His people. Here we are wedded to Christ who is the Light of the World, the Word of God, the Living Water, and the Bread of Life.

This accomplishment of the Easter Vigil is also the goal of the Easter Season, the period of fifty days of special peace and joy for all disciples of Christ. And as I suggested earlier, the Easter Vigil serves as a microcosm of the entire Christian life, for isn't that our goal—to be as completely one with the Lord as possible? We achieve this in our lives through prayer, by keeping the commandments, by our membership in the Christian community, by serving others, and especially by participating in the sacramental life of the Church. Our whole life then becomes a living out of the mysteries proclaimed and realized in the Easter Vigil.

In the poem "Easter Vigil 1966" by Karol Wojtyla, now Pope John Paul II, we see the convergence of death and life that occurs in the Easter Vigil. Through powerful sign and symbol, we return to the place where Jesus died, but in fact, to the place where He was born anew. Easter is a time of new birth, a moment in which we stand in front of the glory-filled future we expect as Christians.

Thy Liberty with Law

America! America!
God mend thine ev'ry flaw,
Confirm thy soul in self-control
Thy liberty in law.

Every Fourth of July we hear lots of patriotic songs. Without a doubt my favorite is "America the Beautiful." It's much easier to sing than the National Anthem and has beautiful lyrics, words that extol the blessings of our nation and challenge us to live up to the vision of our founders. The words quoted above, for example, allow a place for God in the life of our country; they extol the virtue of self-control and strike a fine balance between the blessing of liberty and the responsibility of law.

Independence Day! America is "the land of the free," and we rightly cherish our freedom. The commitment to freedom and equality is deeply etched in our national psyche. Americans have bravely fought and died to defend the freedom we treasure today. We should always be grateful to those courageous men and women who made generous sacrifices to ensure the freedom of this nation and its citizens.

But freedom is much more than a national treasure or a political right. It is a human right, given to mankind by God Himself. The Second Vatican Council taught that it is "only in freedom that man can turn himself towards what is good. . . . But that which is truly freedom is an exceptional sign of the image of God in man" (*Gaudium et Spes*, no. 17). Throughout the world today, led by the fearless voice of Pope John Paul II, the Church is the champion of human rights, dignity, and freedom as inalienable gifts of God.

However, there are certain trends in society today that exaggerate the nature of freedom and in doing so threaten the very freedom they seek to defend. How quickly we forget that there is no such thing as absolute freedom, that every freedom is accompanied by responsibility.

Again we turn to the pope to illustrate this concept. In his masterful 1993 encyclical, *Veritatis Splendor* (The Splendor of Truth), the pope explains why man's freedom is not unlimited:

> [Freedom] must halt before the "tree of the knowledge of good and evil," for it is called to accept the moral law given by God. In fact, human freedom finds its authentic and complete fulfillment precisely in the acceptance of that law. God, who alone is good, knows perfectly what is good for man, and by virtue of his very love proposed this good to man in the commandments (no. 35).

Freedom is always circumscribed by the moral law. Any expression of freedom is obligated to respect the common good and the rights of other people. Liberty is not license. There is no freedom without a corresponding accountability. While these might seem like vague philosophical principles, they result in very practical, everyday consequences.

Any parent who has ever handed over the car keys to a teenage son understands these principles. While the teenager wants to spread his wings and enjoy more freedom, he also assumes a greater responsibility for his actions and for the well-being and safety of others. If he abuses his new freedom and drives carelessly, he loses the right to drive. The car stays in the garage and the teenager in his room.

It seems to me that our nation is presently struggling with several important issues related to the concepts of freedom and responsibility. Permit me to mention just two.

Let's talk about freedom of speech, a fundamental freedom enshrined in the law of the land. We certainly have the right to speak and write what we believe, to express our opinions without fear of recrimination. But freedom of speech has its limits. The law established a long time ago that you are not free to shout "fire" in a theater. Nor are you free to incite a riot, intimidate members of racial or religious groups, use obscenities on the radio, or threaten the life of the President. If you do so you are subject to punishment, for you have stepped beyond the boundaries of free speech as defined by the law. Try talking about the bomb in your suitcase the next time you're boarding a plane, and as you're hauled away, protest that you were just exercising your right of free speech!

The question is, where do we draw the line? Shouldn't there be limits around free speech when it threatens moral harm as well as physical harm? Isn't it legitimate to have certain boundaries around the "speech" that occurs in art, music, the media, and the Internet if these forms of expression undermine the moral health of our children or society in general? Who has exempted these means of self-expression from the moral law? Censorship is often considered an evil concept, but there is a legitimate place for "censorship" if it protects people from the abuse of unbridled "free speech."

And what about guns? The Constitution speaks about the right to "bear arms," although the purpose of that phrase is often debated. Disregarding the apparent intention of the Constitution, some reject *any* restrictions on the sale, owner-ship, and use of firearms, insisting that they have the "right," or freedom, to do whatever they want.

But, I ask, at what price do they exercise their alleged freedom? Doesn't the proliferation of guns in our homes and neighborhoods and the increase of violence in society argue for some limits, some reasonable restraints? I know, I know . . . "Guns don't kill people, people kill people," the tiresome saying insists. But the fact is that people use guns more than any other weapon to kill people. In thinking of the terrible violence that has occurred in schools over the last few years, I can't recall even one case in which students were stabbed or bludgeoned to death by a crazed classmate. The right to buy, own, and use guns is not an absolute right. It is, as it must be, limited to the common good of society and the need to protect others.

These same principles can be applied in a similar fashion to any freedom in our nation, including the so-called "freedom of choice" that results in the plague of abortion. Even freedom of religion has its limits in a democratic society.

In his beautiful homily in Baltimore in 1995, Pope John Paul II summed up the essential relationship between freedom and moral responsibility. He asked:

> The basic question before a democratic society is, "How ought we to live together?" In seeking an answer to this question, can society exclude moral truth and moral reasoning? Can the biblical wisdom which played such a formative part in the very founding of your country be excluded from that debate? Would not doing so mean that America's founding documents no longer have any defining content, but are only the formal dressing of changing opinion? . . . Surely it is important for America that the moral truths which make freedom possible should be passed on to each generation. Every generation of Americans needs to know that freedom consists not in doing what we like, but in having the right to do what we ought.

As we celebrate our independence on the Fourth of July, let's thank God for the bountiful blessings He has bestowed upon our land, blessings we often take for granted. Let us be especially grateful for the gift of freedom. But let us also remember that for each of us, and for our nation, there is no freedom without responsibility. America, confirm thy soul in self-control, thy liberty in law.

An Open Letter to College Students

Dear college student,

Whether you are about to begin college for the first time or are returning to continue your studies, this is an important and challenging time in your life. On this occasion I'd like to share a few thoughts with you. I wish I could meet you personally, but that's not possible. Nonetheless, I hope you will accept my reflections in the spirit they're given, a spirit of sincerity and love.

As you begin, or continue, your higher education, I hope, first of all, that you will be aware of and grateful for all the blessings you've already received from Almighty God. You live in freedom, in a nation where it is possible for you to pursue the education of your choice, to have your hopes and dreams fulfilled. God has blessed you with material prosperity, health, intelligence, and talent. Chances are you've been supported by loving parents and surrounded by a family and many friends who really care for you. You've been given the opportunity to acquire a solid education that will serve as the foundation of your future success. (Now you'll find out why you spent all those hours learning reading and spelling, science and math!)

Most importantly, you've been blessed with the gift of your Catholic faith, and I pray that you'll always treasure that gift. Your faith has introduced you to God, enriched your life, made you a better person, and given you a clear moral framework from which to make good, constructive decisions about life.

Now you must be prepared, perhaps for the first time in your life, to have your faith tested. On your campus and during your studies, you will meet people who have values very different from yours, or perhaps no values at all. Some people will question your faith, ridicule your faith, and shake the very moral and spiritual foundations on which you've built your entire life. When this happens, be confident, be strong, and be faithful. Be proud of your Catholic heritage and remember that "Catholic" is something you *are*, not something you *do*!

It's essential that you continue learning about your faith so that you can give solid answers to questions you encounter. And your faith needs to be lived every day if it is to prosper at this challenging time. Your newfound freedom presumes additional personal responsibility, and that includes the regular practice of your religious faith.

So, be sure to attend Mass on Sundays and holy days and receive Holy Communion. God has given you 168 hours each week for your own use and asks just one of those in return for Himself. Regularly use the Sacrament of Reconciliation. Good Confessions will keep you on the right path. Develop a personal prayer life that will keep you in touch with God every day—not just during final exam time! Listen attentively to the Word of God as it is preached, and read the Bible on your own. The Word of God will give you much support and direction. And develop a devotion to the Blessed Mother and your patron saint. They will be your constant companions on your life's journey.

It would be very helpful for you to get involved in the local Catholic Newman Center or campus ministry at your college or university, where you will find other young people who share your values. The campus ministry leaders will really welcome your presence and encourage your participation. Also, stay in touch with your parish back home. You have lots of friends and spiritual support there, too.

And speaking of values, strive to hang on to those good Christian values you've learned at home and Church, values such as respect for human life (you'll have plenty of opportunities to defend it!); integrity and honesty in your personal and public life; a commitment to Christian marriage and family life; concern for the poor, weak, and disadvantaged; and the desire to be a compassionate, forgiving, and peaceful person.

Scrupulously avoid the evil temptations that are part of society today, temptations that are especially attractive to young people. Avoid addictions—to drugs, alcohol, tobacco, money, work, and the Internet—they are false gods. These addictions are serious distractions to your goals and are loaded with potential problems for you.

Refrain from sexual activity and relationships that are contrary to God's law and your Christian faith. Sex is a beautiful gift of God, an expression of life and love so powerful that it is proper only within the stability of a sacramental marriage. Have good friends and surround yourself with people who share your values. Stay away from those who will lead you astray and pull you down. Again, remember that your new freedom is wonderful, but demands a renewed commitment to act responsibly.

Even at this time when you are rightly focused on your future, be generous, sharing your material, personal, and spiritual gifts with others. Volunteer your time to help others, at college, in your community, and for the Church. Carefully consider a life of service in the Church, particularly in the religious life or priesthood. It is a rich and fulfilling vocation, and the Church needs good young people like you to carry on its mission in the world. Pray over this question: "What has God created me to do with my life on earth?" And be open to the answer you receive, wherever that answer may lead you.

A word about technology, which is already a well-established part of your routine. On campus and in the classroom, you will be surrounded by the latest advances in technology and communications. (When I was in college it was an innovation for the school to have a computer, much less every student!) The increasing reliance on technology is fraught with danger, but properly used is a wonderful resource.

Even with the most advanced technology, however, and perhaps because of it, you will have to work hard to become a good communicator. Learn to speak and write clearly and effectively; no machine can do that for you. Even more importantly, learn to listen to others, not only with your ears, but with your heart. Appreciate the diversity of other people and respect their points of view, without compromising your own beliefs. Listening is essential to the building of solid relationships now and in the future.

Remember that your education is a tool to prepare you for the service of humanity and not just a means of making money and accumulating material possessions. You will discover that there are certain objective truths in life, concrete moral guidelines that are unchangeable. Not everything is subjective. Not everything is relative to your own personal interpretation.

As Pope John Paul II has written, "Faith and reason are like two wings on which the human spirit rises to the contemplation of the truth . . . in a word, to know [God] himself" (*Fides et Ratio*). In other terms, all truth leads ultimately to God. Faith and knowledge go hand in hand. Faith without knowledge is not grounded in reality; knowledge without faith is sterile and incomplete.

So, dear friend, as you are about to begin, or resume, your college career, this very important chapter in your life's story, please know that you will have a special place in my prayers. I hope you will pray for me and for the whole Church, too!

Take full advantage of your college experience, learn a lot, and have the time of your life. But stay grounded in the God who created you and has been so very good to you. Remain committed to your Catholic faith. Regardless of how much you accomplish in the future, you will be a better person if your faith is an integral part of your life!

Sincerely yours,
Bishop Tobin

Are You Working Too Hard?

I've always thought of Labor Day as a bittersweet holiday, a day of mixed signals and emotions. The last of the three great summer holidays, it marks the end of summer, even though some of the finest weather of the year is yet to come. It means returning to school, even for the students whose classes have already begun. Students won't really be present, not really, until after Labor Day. Labor Day heralds shorter days and longer nights and the change of seasons.

Labor Day is primarily a civil holiday and a social event, but it has also taken on religious significance, at least in Catholic circles. The Church uses the occasion to reaffirm its teaching about the dignity and value of workers and the work they do. We recall that work is not an end in itself, but rather a participation in God's work of creation and redemption, as our labors are intended to hasten the coming of God's kingdom on earth. The Scriptures and the Tradition of the Church remind us that every person has a right and duty to work, that workers deserve just compensation and safe working conditions, and that our work is directed to the benefit of our families, our community, our nation, and all the people of the world.

The Christian observance of Labor Day also teaches us that how we do our work is as important as the specific kind of work we do. Every task, however menial in human terms, has true and lasting value if done for the right reason and with the proper intention. "[W]hatever you do . . ." Saint Paul says, "do everything in the name of the Lord Jesus" (Col. 3:17). Every work should be our personal response to God's call in our life: not merely a job or profession, but a true vocation. Conversely, even the most religious of activities loses its value if not done for the right motives.

There are consequences to this Christian vision of labor. Whenever we define our work in terms of creation, redemption, and the kingdom of God, we accept the premise that work involves the cooperation of God and man. But at that point of convergence, one of two heresies can begin to enter the picture.

The first heresy is to pretend that everything depends on God, and this leads to the abdication of all human responsibility for the condition of the world. We can become so concerned with the rewards of the next life that we choose to ignore the responsibilities of the present.

The other heresy, however, is much more prevalent in our age. I'm speaking of the temptation to believe, perhaps even subconsciously, that we alone are responsible for creation, redemption, and kingdom building. Thus we attempt to carry the burden by ourselves and quickly lose sight of the presence and power of God. This leads inevitably to one of the dominant sins of our age—workaholism.

It seems that especially in our American culture, we have become addicted to work. We no longer take time to rest, relax, and recreate, though it is clear that the Lord wants us to. We have become obsessed with productivity, and we equate the amount of our work with the validation of our worth. We've lost sight of other values in the process. Our health has suffered, our families have suffered, and the practice of our faith has suffered. Our progress as a human family has been stymied because our human needs have been ignored.

There are many manifestations of our addiction. Professionals feel obliged to work fifty, sixty, and seventy hours a week to "get ahead" or "stay ahead." Both parents enter the workplace, not always because they have to, but because their lifestyle demands it or because they feel guilty about the free time they have. People sleep in their offices overnight so that they can start earlier in the morning. And they wonder why their children don't know them.

The development of technology has backfired. Remember the prediction that communication systems and computer technology would allow us to have more leisure time and thus be able to enjoy the finer things of life—nature, poetry, music, travel, and prayer?

Instead, our expertise has enabled us to work constantly. We have telephones and computers on our patios, in our cars, and in our golf carts. I recently read that one country club had to finally ban telephones in golf carts because their ringing was disturbing other golfers who were trying to concentrate on their game. I thought that golf was supposed to be recreation, a time to get away from the office.

We can travel faster, and so we travel farther. We attend conferences, seminars, and workshops across the nation and around the world. We travel to high-tech programs aimed at increasing our work efficiency, a problem that wouldn't exist if we stayed home more often!

Workaholism. The Church is not immune to this virus either. What would the Church today do without meetings? Given my own schedule, I am destined to die someday in a conference room. Oh for the day that there was at least a chance that I would succumb on a golf course!

It seems that the Universal Church, the diocesan Church, and parishes too are caught up in bureaucracy and worka-holism. I'm told that it is not unusual for parish meetings to be held in rectories until 10:00 and 11:00 p.m. We've come to the point where we talk about prayer in a meeting room, rather than actually praying in the church. We keep parents of young children at the parish all night to plan programs to strengthen the quality of family life!

We no longer rest. Isn't it ironic that Labor Day, a national holiday to reward workers, will find many people working in stores that feel obliged to ruin the free day? We have all-night sales and special sales on Sundays to lure people out of the comfort of their homes and thus increase ever so slightly the profit margin. Convenience stores are open twenty-four hours a day because, for some reason, people find it convenient to shop at three or four o'clock in the morning.

Is it all worth it? When we reach our final resting place (the concept of "resting place" sounds more attractive all the time), will we have made the best possible use of our limited time on earth, or will we have simply worked our way through it? As one sage observed, "I've never heard anyone on his deathbed say, 'I wish I had spent more time at the office.'"

Labor Day is indeed a time to proclaim the dignity of the laborer and the value of the work we do. It is a time to celebrate the fact that God has called us to be partners in the work of creation and redemption. But it is also a time, I believe, to admit that sometimes we take ourselves too seriously and that we have forced God out of the picture.

As we celebrate Labor Day, we should pause to remember that to be fully human, we need time to rest, relax, recreate, and pray. Jesus, who had the weight of the whole world on His shoulders, was able to say to His disciples, "Come away by yourselves to a lonely place, and rest a while" (Mk. 6:31). Perhaps it is time for us to accept the Lord's invitation. Why not today?

Angel of God

Angel of God, my guardian dear,
To whom God's love commits me here.
Ever this day be at my side
To light and guard, to rule and guide.

Generations of Catholics have learned this beautiful prayer to our guardian angels, and it seems especially appropriate during October, a time of particular devotion to the angels in heaven.

Actually, as a prelude to the month of the angels, we celebrate the feast of the great archangels, Michael, Gabriel, and Raphael, on September 29. The Office of Readings that day contains a homily on the topic by Pope Saint Gregory the Great, written in the sixth century:

> You should be aware that the word "angel" denotes a function rather than a nature. Those holy spirits of heaven have indeed always been spirits. They can only be called angels when they deliver some message. Moreover, those who deliver messages of lesser importance are called angels; and those who proclaim messages of supreme importance are called archangels.
>
> Some angels are given proper names to denote the service they are empowered to perform. Thus Michael means, "Who is like God"; Gabriel is "The Strength of God"; and Raphael is "God's Remedy."

Belief in spiritual creatures called angels is an important part of our Catholic tradition. During the Profession of Faith at Mass, we proclaim our belief in God, the Creator of "all that is seen and unseen." The Catechism explains the Church's teaching concerning angels in more detail:

> The existence of spiritual, non-corporeal beings that Sacred Scripture usually calls "angels" is a truth of faith. The witness of Scripture is as clear as the unanimity of Tradition (no. 328).

> As purely *spiritual* creatures angels have intelligence and will: they are personal and immortal creatures, surpassing in perfection all visible creatures, as the splendor of their glory bears witness (no. 330, original emphasis).

> Christ is the center of the angelic world. They are *his* angels. . . . From the Incarnation to the Ascension, the life of the Word incarnate is surrounded by the adoration and service of angels. . . . They protect Jesus in his infancy, serve him in the desert, strengthen him in his agony in the garden. . . . They will be present at Christ's return, which they will announce, to serve at his judgment (nos. 331, 333).

> In the meantime, the whole life of the Church benefits from the mysterious and powerful help of angels. In her liturgy, the Church joins with the angels to adore the thrice-holy God (nos. 334-35).

And what about guardian angels, whose feast we celebrate on October 2? I remember our teachers in Catholic grade school having us slide over in our seats to make room for our guardian angels to sit beside us. While I don't recall how long this accommodation was observed, nor how many kids fell out of their seats, the impact was real.

The Catechism reminds us of the role of our guardian angels: "From its beginning until death, human life is surrounded by their watchful care and intercession. Beside each believer stands an angel as protector and shepherd leading him to life" (no. 336).

On October 2, the Liturgy of the Hours contains another beautiful passage, this time by Saint Bernard, describing the powerful assistance of our guardian angels:

> *He has given his angels charge over you to guard you in all your ways.* These words should fill you with respect, inspire devotion and instill confidence; respect for the presence of angels, devotion because of their loving service, and confidence because of their protection. And so the angels are here; they are at your side, they are with you, present on your behalf. . . .
>
> We should, then, my brothers, show our affection for the angels, for one day they will be our coheirs just as here below they are our guardians and trustees appointed and set over us by the Father. . . .
>
> Even though we are children and have a long, a very long and dangerous way to go, with such protectors what have we to fear? . . . They are loyal, prudent, and powerful. Why then are we afraid?

I must confess, as perhaps you do too, that most of the time in my daily life I'm rather oblivious to the angel at my side. But maybe the month of October is a chance to correct that neglect. As we consider and pray to the angels, what are some of the practical lessons we can learn?

The first is the reality of the spiritual world. We say we believe in things "visible and invisible," but in fact our lives seem to be completely focused on the visible things. The existence of angels and our devotion to them causes us to remember that an important part of creation is invisible to the human eye. Though we can't see them, at least not very often, angels are real, as are devils. They need to be taken very seriously.

The pope emphasized this truth in a recent series of talks about the afterlife. He taught that heaven, hell, and purgatory aren't so much "places" as relationships between us and God. Some people are very upset over this teaching, though it's certainly not new. But the fact that heaven, hell, and purgatory aren't simply physical places doesn't mean they are any less real. They truly exist and will serve as "destinations" for us after our life on earth.

Further, angels are a manifestation of the powerful presence and providence of God in our daily lives. The angels, as messengers, guardians, and guides, have been sent by God and they speak to us of God's constant love. Think in these terms: Through the angels God provides spiritual day care for His children.

A couple years ago I received a letter from a student preparing for Confirmation who made a similar point:

> Dear Bishop Tobin: If I could ask you one question, it would be what you think will happen after the Year 2000 and with Y2K. In my opinion, we should be relying on each other and our own faith rather than on computers, because computers will let you down and our faith and our friends will not.

Well said, my young friend! Our faith in God is crucial to a peaceful and productive life. God is always present to us and we can indeed always depend on Him. God will not fail in the new millennium. The ministry of angels is a guarantee that God is on our side, that we have nothing to fear.

Finally, the celebration of angels leads us right back to earth again and reminds us that we need also to take care of ourselves and to be "angels" to one another. The reality of God's providence does not excuse us from human responsibility. Even the power of angels can't prevent us from getting into trouble—material or spiritual—if we are determined to do so. Angels won't protect us on the highway if we insist on driving carelessly. And all the angels in the universe can't preserve us from sin if we freely and frequently place ourselves in dangerous moral situations.

We need to take care of others, too, and be "human angels" in that sense. For example, we should always be messengers, announcing the Gospel of Christ to others by our words and deeds. Through our commitment to justice and charity, we can extend God's care as surely as the angels do. And our good example of a Christian life well lived can lead others to spiritual safety and out of harm's way.

Let us conclude this reflection on angels, then, as we began, with prayer:

God our Father, in your loving providence you send your holy angels to watch over us. Hear our prayers, defend us always by their protection, and let us share your life with them forever. Amen.

Souls of the Just

I don't exercise as much as I used to, or should. When I do exercise, I enjoy walking, and very often I walk through cemeteries. Some might find this weird. I find it relaxing. Cemeteries are usually quiet and safe. Walking in a cemetery reminds me of the shortness of my own life and helps to keep the trials and tribulations of everyday life in proper perspective. While I walk in a cemetery, I pray for those who are buried there.

During the month of November, the Church also takes a spiritual walk through its cemetery as we remember and pray for all those who have died. Our devotion to the faithful departed is a beautiful and important part of our Catholic heritage.

The foundation of this observance is our belief in the "Communion of Saints." The Church is more than just the assembly of the faithful on earth; it includes the saints in heaven and the souls in purgatory.

November begins with the celebration of All Saints Day, a beautiful feast, a holy day of obligation for Catholics. On this day the Church rejoices with our brothers and sisters who are in heaven, those who have successfully completed their journey on earth and now enjoy the blessed company of the angels and saints. The observance of All Saints Day gives us joy, hope, and encouragement, for we look to that day when we too will be numbered among the saints. We admire the saints for their example and we beg for their prayers on our behalf.

November 2 is All Souls Day, a more somber observance, yet one that is filled with quiet hope and gratitude. On this day we reflect upon and pray for those who have died but have not yet entered the kingdom of heaven. This observance is continued through the month of November. There are both theological and personal reasons why this practice is so valuable.

The Church has taught, and continues to teach, the existence of purgatory. The word "purgatory" itself means "a place for purging, a place for purifying." The Catechism reminds us:

> All who die in God's grace and friendship, but still imperfectly purified, are indeed assured of their eternal salvation; but after death they undergo purification, so as to achieve holiness necessary to enter the joy of heaven.
>
> The Church gives the name *Purgatory* to this final purification of the elect, which is entirely different from the punishment of the damned. . . .
>
> From the beginning the Church has honored the memory of the dead and offered prayers in suffrage for them, above all the Eucharistic sacrifice, so that, thus purified, they may attain the beatific vision of God. The Church also commends almsgiving, indulgences, and works of penance undertaken on behalf of the dead (nos. 1030-32, original emphasis).

Some people don't believe in the existence of purgatory, but to me it makes great sense. The need for purgatory is entirely consistent with the reality of the human condition, isn't it? We live on earth, we try to be good and do good, but often fail. When we die, how can we who are imperfect be completely united to God who is perfect? Purgatory deals with our imperfection and prepares us, finally, for eternal life.

And it is only because of purgatory that it makes any sense to pray for the dead. There is no need to pray for the saints in heaven; they have received their final reward. There is no purpose in praying for those in hell; their judgment is final, and our prayers are of no avail. Only purgatory justifies our prayers for the dead.

But what of the more personal reasons for praying for the dead? One of the most precious aspects of our Catholic tradition is our love and reverence for those who have died. We remember them and pray for them because they are our ancestors in faith, because they have made us what we are and have given us the good that we have.

In a special way, of course, we think of the members of our families who have died. Our families have given us life and love; very often they have suffered and sacrificed much for us. They have bestowed upon us our Christian faith, have taught us about right and wrong, have instilled in us important values, and have shown us how to live good, productive, and enjoyable lives. How could we ever forget them? How good it is to pray for the dead. November is a time to remember and say "thank you" in a prayerful and spiritual way.

November is also a fitting occasion to recall the importance of being spiritually prepared for death. Death is a reality that touches every living person; it is also a sublime Christian mystery. The Catechism says:

> The dying should be given attention and care to help them live their last moments in dignity and peace. They will be helped by the prayer of their relatives, who must see to it that the sick receive at the proper time the sacraments that prepare them to meet the living God (no. 2299).

Finally, it is good to emphasize the importance of Catholic funerals and burials. These sacred traditions are increasingly challenged by an ever-changing, ever-expanding secular and corporate funeral industry. Even faithful Catholics are being lured away from beautiful, traditional Catholic practices by the promise of convenience and frugality.

Catholic tradition and practice maintains the following: Catholic funerals should be celebrated with the Mass and normally take place in a Catholic parish church; in-ground burials in Catholic cemeteries or use of Catholic mausoleums is preferred by the Church; cremation is permitted only if it doesn't intend to deny the teachings of the Church about death and resurrection; cremains (ashes of those cremated) must be respectfully buried and not taken home as a mantelpiece or scattered on favorite beaches or golf courses. Remember that these ashes have been anointed in Christ and have housed the Holy Spirit of God. They should never be treated playfully or irreverently.

Saint Paul says that "if we have been united with [Christ] in a death like his, we shall certainly be united with him in a resurrection like his" (Rom. 6:5). Our approach to death and burial, like our approach to life itself, is an expression of our faith, always prayerful, spiritual, Christian, and Catholic.

So, let us remember in November. Let us remember with love those who have gone before us in death. Let us pray for the peaceful repose of their souls:

Lord our God, the death of our brothers and sisters recalls our human condition and the brevity of our lives on earth. But for those who believe in your love, death is not the end, nor does it destroy the bonds that you forge in our lives. We share the faith of your Son's disciples and the hope of the children of God. Bring the light of Christ's Resurrection as we pray for those we love. Amen.

III

Serving God's People

Seven Things You Should Know

What exactly does it mean to be a Catholic today? This question, in its many forms, always generates a lively discussion, at least in religious circles. Individuals wrestle with this question, as do hospitals, colleges, and newspapers. Without even trying to answer this complex question, I would like to propose seven things every Catholic should know about being Catholic in the world today:

(1) **Not all religions are the same.** When I was a kid, I used to worry about my non-Catholic friends because I wasn't sure they could ever be saved. Although it was never a teaching of the Church, it was a common perception, perhaps just a "feeling," that only Catholics went to heaven. We know, of course, that's not true and that one's salvation depends more on the state of one's conscience than on any specific religious affiliation.

Nonetheless, it seems to me that today we've gone to the other extreme. How often have we heard it said, "All religions are the same," or "We all worship the same God, so what's the difference?" In fact, there are very real differences among religions and denominations. Catholics have certain beliefs and practices that aren't shared by Lutherans, Episcopalians, Baptists, or Methodists. Even in this very ecumenical age, we need to affirm that there is something very special about being Catholic. We should be aware of it and proud of it.

(2) **The Church is human.** I am convinced that most people who leave the Church do so not because they disagree with the

teachings or discipline of the Church, but rather for human reasons—they've had an argument with their pastor, they disagree with their child's teacher, or they are scandalized by the gossip spread by their fellow Catholics. The Church is, has always been, and will always be thoroughly human. All you have to do to be reminded of that truth is read the headlines. The Church is human because it is composed of real, imperfect human beings like you and me. When we come into the Church, we bring with us all of our sins, weaknesses, and needs. Isn't that why we begin every Eucharistic liturgy asking for God's forgiveness?

As someone said, if you find a perfect church out there somewhere, by all means join it—but remember, the moment you join it, it will cease being perfect!

(3) **The Church is divine.** When we focus too much on the human dimension of the Church, we can easily lose sight of her other dimension. The Church is also divine! We believe that the Church was established by Jesus Christ, the Son of God, and continues to be guided by the Holy Spirit.

Therefore, the Church is much more than just another fraternal organization or social club. The Church is a manifestation of the People of God and the Body of Christ. That's why it's so important that we always approach the Church with a great deal of reverence and respect. True Catholics don't sue the Church; they don't teach heresy and error; they don't cause public division or scandal. To sin against the Church is to offend the very Body of Christ.

(4) **The works of the Church are a combination of human and divine.** Sometimes we take ourselves too seriously. We take on too much responsibility for our own redemption. From the perspective of salvation history, even in the relatively brief history of the Church on earth, you and I are only one small

part of the whole, at one brief moment in time. The Church was here long before us and will survive long after we are gone. Despite the best, and sometimes the worst, of our human efforts, God is still in charge of the Church and the world.

In everything we do, therefore, we ask for God's assistance. When we work for vocations, religious education, human life, or social justice, or whatever we undertake in the name of the Church, we strive to do our very best and then let God do the rest. That's why prayer is such an important part of our human endeavors.

(5) **Being Catholic means being different.** Do your friends know that you are a Catholic? Do they recognize you as a disciple of Christ? Are you different enough to be noticed? When Jesus told His disciples to be the "salt of the earth" and the "light of the world," He was telling them to be different from their environment, to relate to the world, and to make a difference in the quality of the world.

If we are truly Catholic, we will often find that we are different from the world around us, especially in our religious practices and moral values. This is evident, for example, in our approach to the Sacrament of Matrimony and human sexuality, in our commitment to human life, in our compassion for the poor and disadvantaged. Often the world will reject our teachings and ridicule us personally. So be it. That's what the world did to Jesus. What is important is not that we are popular or socially acceptable, but that we are faithful.

(6) **Your membership in the Church transcends your parish.** Your membership and active participation in your parish are extremely important. There you will most often practice your faith, and there your faith will be nourished by the preaching of the Gospel, the reception of the sacraments, and the support of a caring community.

In allegiance to their parishes, however, some Catholics become myopic and lose sight of the bigger picture. Always keep in mind that being Catholic means that you are part of a reality greater than your parish. If your parish closes or you move out of town, you're still a Catholic. You belong to a particular diocese and to the Universal Church in Rome. Without the Universal Church there would be no diocese; without a diocese there would be no parish. While this truth has tangible expressions such as diocesan and national collections and programs, it is primarily a spiritual reality, rooted in the nature of the Church herself.

(7) **Who owns the Church?** Sometimes you will hear a preacher or teacher say, "This is *your* Church!" When you hear those words, hang onto your wallets and purses, for almost invariably when someone says, "This is your Church," he's looking for a contribution of money or time.

Who owns the Church? Even though civil law and canon law affirm that the bishop owns Church property, the bishop doesn't own the Church. The pope doesn't own the Church. And neither do you. In truth, Christ owns the Church. He bought her and paid for her with the price of His own blood. He established the Church, nourished the Church, prayed for the Church, and died for the Church. And He gave her to us to take care of, each according to our particular position and role within the Church. It is a sacred trust, an awesome responsibility which the Lord has given to us.

What does it mean to be Catholic today? It means many things, of course. The Church is a mystery to be embraced, a reality to be lived, a gift for which we should be eternally grateful.

If I may repeat some words from my homily of February 2, 1996, when I was installed as Bishop of Youngstown:

Honesty and truth require that anyone, any person or agency, that assumes the name "Catholic" must be authentically Roman Catholic. And what does that mean, but that we are united to the Universal Church; that we love, respect, and obey the Holy Father, the Vicar of Christ on earth; that we accept and promote all the teachings of the Church; that we live a moral life in sacramental and structural communion with the Church; that we are proud of our Catholic heritage and anxious to pass that heritage on to future generations.

Every person or agency that bears the name Catholic, whether it be a Catholic parish, a Catholic high school, a Catholic university, a Catholic hospital, a Catholic social agency, a Catholic newspaper, or a Catholic cemetery, is called to be authentically Roman Catholic, embracing everything that noble name implies.

The Gift of Faith

Ultimately, faith is the only key to the universe. The final meaning of human existence, and the answers to the questions on which all our happiness depends, cannot be found in any other way.

—Thomas Merton

Faith is the "yes" of individuals to God. It is their "amen." Faith helps us discover the signs of God's loving presence in creation, in people, in the events of history, and above all, in the work and message of Christ.

—Pope John Paul II

If you have faith as a grain of mustard seed, you will say to this mountain, "Move hence to yonder place," and it will move; and nothing will be impossible to you.

—Jesus of Nazareth

What does faith mean for you? Is it simply a lifesaver God throws to you during the turbulent times of life, or is it a reality that influences all of your activities and experiences?

It seems to me that our Catholic faith is one of the many gifts we often take for granted. There are times, I know, when we are more attuned to the importance of faith, our total dependence on God's providence. In times such as serious illness, the death of a loved one, a personal crisis, or national tragedy, we turn quickly to God, pleading for His comfort and help. But as soon as the crisis subsides and we return to our normal routine, God is once again relegated to the corner, taking His quiet place next to the fire extinguisher we all have but hope to never use.

If our faith is to have validity or importance, shouldn't it be one of the primary building blocks of our life? Shouldn't it influence all of our experiences? After all, as Thomas Merton observed, it is only in faith we can find the answers to "the questions on which all of our happiness depends."

The question, then, is this: How does your faith affect your daily life?

First, does your faith result in the active and enthusiastic practice of religion? Although faith and religion are distinct, they are closely related. Does your faith inspire you to participate in Holy Mass on Sundays and holy days of obligation and receive the sacraments of the Church regularly? Are you an enthusiastic Catholic or a nominal Catholic, doing only what you need to do to fulfill your basic obligations? (When was the last time you attended Mass because you *wanted* to and not because you *had* to?) Are you raising your children in the faith and giving them a good example in your daily life? What is your attitude toward the Church? Are you often critical of the Church, her teachings and leaders, or do you respect the Church as the Body of Christ, led by the Spirit of God?

Second, does your faith influence the living out of your vocation? Are you faithful to your marriage vows, seeking always to deepen your covenant of life and love? Are you receptive to new life in your marriage, welcoming the children God sends you, or have you bought into the contraceptive mentality of our age?

If you are a priest or deacon, do you bring a spirit of joy and enthusiasm to your ministry, or is the idealism and zeal of your ordination day just a distant memory? If you are a consecrated religious, does your faith translate into the sincere desire for personal spiritual growth, into a faithful living out of the vows of poverty, chastity, and obedience, or has your lifestyle become so secular that it's no longer recognizable as an expression of consecrated life?

Next, does your religious faith motivate an authentic commitment to charity and justice? As Saint James reminds us so pointedly:

> What does it profit, my brethren, if a man says he has faith but has not works? Can his faith save him? If a brother or sister is ill-clad and in lack of daily food, and one of you says to them, "Go in peace, be warmed and filled," without giving them the things needed for the body, what does it profit? So faith by itself, if it has no works, is dead (Jas. 2:14-17).

How do you respond to the needs of the poor? Do you really try to understand their plight and learn about the causes of poverty in the world today? How do you speak of the poor—in an understanding, compassionate manner, or in a condescending, judgmental way? Do you share your material resources and participate in collections and local programs that help the poor? Is there some provision for the Church and charity in your will, so that even in your passing your worldly possessions will bring about some lasting good?

Another point: How does your faith in God affect the development of your moral character? Do you diligently follow the commandments of the Lord regarding reverence for sacred things, respect for the personal property of others, the dignity of human sexuality and human life, and the good name and reputation of others? Is your professional life marked by integrity, or do you "get away with as much as possible" in the hope of not getting caught? Do you live the virtues of reconciliation and forgiveness in your personal relationships, or are you one to harbor anger and bitterness when someone harms you? Is there a spirit of humility in your life, or do you envy others, always insist on being number one, and always demand to have your own way?

And how does your faith guide you when you *can't* have your own way, when you're not in control of the circumstances of life? Are you as friendly to God during the difficult times as you are during the good? When you are required to suffer, do you become angry, bitter, and withdrawn, or are you able to find some meaning, some value in your suffering? Do you try to follow God's will even when it requires of you something unpleasant or exceedingly difficult?

In the context of faith, the many experiences of life conspire to teach us the wisdom of the words of Jesus:

> If any man would come after me, let him deny himself and take up his cross and follow me. For whoever would save his life will lose it; and whoever loses his life for my sake and the gospel's will save it (Mk. 8:34-35).

As we saw at the beginning of this section, there are many definitions and descriptions of faith. But it all comes down to this: Faith is our freely chosen response to God who creates us, loves us, saves us, and at our lives' end will judge us. Faith is a commitment that touches every aspect of our existence.

A young lady preparing for Confirmation wrote to me to explain what Confirmation meant for her, why she wanted to be confirmed, and how she had grown in the understanding of her faith. In a beautiful and heartfelt expression, she wrote the following:

> I would like to tell you what Confirmation means to me. As an infant I was baptized. I was brought up by Christian parents and raised to love Jesus. I went to Sunday school as a kid, and in second grade I received my First Communion.
>
> I am now about to receive Confirmation. The sacraments I received in the past were due to my parents' belief. My parents chose to baptize me, and they chose to give me First Communion. But now it is my say. When receiving Confirmation you are given the opportunity to say, "Yes, I am a believer." As a baby you depended on your parents.

You'd cry, they'd hold you. When you were hungry, they fed you. As you grew up, though, you became less dependent on your parents and more dependent on yourself.

By receiving Confirmation you are not only showing your parents that you have matured into a beautiful Christian, you are also telling God, "After all this time, you're still number one in my life."

These are fundamental questions to consider. What does faith mean for you? Does it make any significant difference in your life? Is God still number one?

The Questions Kids Ask

A husband and wife invited a number of friends to dinner. At the table the wife turned to their six-year-old daughter and said, "Would you like to say the blessing for us, sweetheart?" "I wouldn't know what to say," replied the little girl. "Just say what you've heard Mommy say," the wife responded. The little girl bowed her head devoutly and said, "Lord, why on earth did I invite all these people to dinner?"

I don't know if the story is true or not, but it is funny. It's also a reminder that "kids say the darnedest things."

They also ask great questions. I've experienced that frequently during my visits to elementary schools in my diocese. Whenever I visit one of our schools, I begin by offering Mass for the students, faculty, and parents, and then spend a good part of the day visiting each classroom. It's then that the fun begins, as I ask the young people questions about religion and they ask me questions about . . . well, almost anything! Let me share with you some of the memorable questions children have asked me.

"Is it fun being a bishop?" This is a common question, and I usually answer it with a sardonic response like, "Yeah, it's a real blast!" The question affords me the opportunity to talk about the ministry of the bishop, and especially how much I enjoy being with the people, visiting our parishes and institutions. It's important to remind the students that they are a part of a Church that is larger than their own parish or school.

"If the pope has a popemobile, do you have a bishopmobile?" The kids are fascinated by the pope, and another question they ask all the time is whether I've met the pope. I explain that I've had the privilege of meeting the pope four or five times, and that it's always very exciting. I remind the children that Pope John Paul II is a great and holy man, and I always ask them to pray for him. By the way, in response to the question, I tell the kids that I don't have a special bishopmobile, just a normal Chevy Lumina. They're always so disappointed!

"How long have you wanted to be a bishop?" Usually I explain that a priest doesn't plan on becoming a bishop, that he is chosen for his position by the pope, and that he really doesn't know that he's going to be a bishop until he receives the surprise announcement. I use this opportunity to share that I did want to be a priest even when I was their age. I also talk about the process of becoming a priest and studying in the seminary. It's an excellent opportunity to remind the students that it is a wonderful thing to serve God in the priesthood and religious life.

"Why do you carry that big cane?" The children always ask about the pastoral staff, the crosier, they saw me use during Mass. The question leads me to talk about being a shepherd. "Who else uses a cane like that?" I ask. "My grandmother," said one young boy. When we got around to talking about shepherds again, I explained that the shepherd's staff has two ends, a pointed end the shepherd uses to get the sheep moving, and a hooked end to keep the sheep from wandering away. I point out that the work of the bishop is somewhat like that, too—to get God's people moving together in the right direction, and to prevent them from wandering away. The kids always ask about the other symbols of the bishop's office they've noticed—the miter, ring, pectoral cross, and zuchetto. "Why do you wear that yarmulke?" asked a lad at Confirmation one evening. "That's not a yarmulke," corrected his mother, "it's a Catholic beanie!"

"Were you on earth when Jesus was alive?" wondered one little girl. I must have looked especially old that day. I think the little girl was really asking, "How do you know Jesus?" In response to the question, I pointed out that Jesus is still alive and with us here on earth, although in a different way than He was 2,000 years ago. The question reminds us that the daily task of the Christian is to recognize the presence of Christ; to know, love, and serve Him; and to share the Good News of Jesus Christ with others.

"Do you ever break the commandments?" asked one inquisitive little boy. I started to explain that since we all are human beings, we all sin and break the commandments . . . but he interrupted me to ask, "Which ones do you break, Bishop?" "I suppose at one time or another I've broken all the commandments," I tried to explain. "You mean you killed someone?" This was a very persistent young man. I always talk to the young people about the commandments, explaining that they are as important today as they were when God gave them to Moses, that if we learn the commandments and keep them, they will lead us to God and prevent us from getting into too much trouble in our lives.

"You mean God owns my tennis shoes?" This question came in the context of a school visit near the Thanksgiving holiday. I had been telling the children that everything we have is a gift from God and that we should be thankful that God has been so good to us. The young man was surprised to learn that his prized possession, his tennis shoes, really belonged to God and were, in effect, only on loan. It is helpful for us to recall once in a while that our gifts do indeed come from a good and loving God, and that we express our gratitude by taking care of our gifts and using them generously in service to others.

"Is our pastor a good priest?" Talk about a loaded question! How could I say no? In truth, the little girl's pastor is a very fine priest, one of the best. But the question reminded me of the critical role priests have in the lives of their people, and how much people, including children, look to their priests as role models and spiritual leaders. The Church is blessed with many outstanding priests, good pastors, good shepherds, who really love and care for the people entrusted to them.

"What is the most challenging part of your work as bishop?" Not all the questions the children ask are funny or lighthearted. Sometimes the older children especially will ask very serious and thought-provoking questions. This question, from a young lady in the eighth grade, prompted me to explain the difficulty of trying to be present to so many people, parishes, and institutions; of trying to constantly reaffirm and build up the people of the Church; of trying to create and share a vision of a Church that is one, holy, catholic, and apostolic. And a great challenge for a bishop—as for any Christian, I suppose—is trying to live up to the vocation we have accepted from God.

"Does your work as bishop ever cause you to be frightened?" What an excellent question, I thought. Without the benefit of much reflection, I responded that there are, indeed, moments when I approach my daily work with a certain amount of fear—especially when I consider the serious responsibility and impressive authority God and the Church have given me, in contrast to my own limitations and human imperfections.

But, as I explained to the young lady who asked the question, and share also with you, dear readers, I am always comforted by the knowledge that I have so much good help and spiritual support throughout my diocese. In the end, I am strengthened by the firm belief that I did not choose this ministry, but that for some inexplicable reason, Christ chose me, and that He will be with me every step of the way.

Matrimony: Is It Still Holy?

Marriage is like a beautiful, gilded bird cage. All the little birds on the outside want to get in, while all the little birds on the inside want to get out!

This saying, by an author unknown to me, summarizes accurately the state of marriage today. Marriage is still an attractive and useful institution, and millions of couples each year begin the journey. At the same time, however, about half of those who enter the "gilded bird cage" find themselves wanting to get out, their marriage ending in separation and divorce.

This poses a real problem for the Church and especially for parish priests who work with engaged couples and witness their vows. This chapter was going to be entitled "Why Priests Hate Weddings," but I thought that might be a bit too strong. Nevertheless, ask any priest about his work, and he will quickly share with you the challenge of dealing with the Sacrament of Marriage today.

The problem, in a nutshell, is that the real practice of weddings and marriage today is far different from the ideal of Holy Matrimony as instituted by Christ and taught by the Church. The Catechism summarizes our teaching about the Sacrament of Matrimony:

> [I]n a Christian marriage the spouses are strengthened and, as it were, consecrated for the duties and the dignity of their state *by a special sacrament.* The consent by which the spouses mutually give and receive one another is sealed by God himself. . . . Authentic married love is caught up into

divine love. . . . This grace proper to the sacrament of Matrimony is intended to perfect the couple's love and to strengthen indissoluble unity. By this grace they "help one another attain holiness in their married life and in welcoming and educating their children" (nos. 1638-1639, 1641, original emphasis, footnotes omitted).

These are lofty and noble words, but in reality priests—and others who assist with marriage preparation—encounter a host of secular challenges in helping couples prepare for the sacrament.

It begins with the fact that so many couples today are living together before they are married. This cohabitation, along with the sexual activity that presumably accompanies it, reveals a lack of understanding about the sanctity of the marital covenant and gives grave scandal to the Christian community.

Many couples who approach the Church for the Sacrament of Matrimony these days do not possess the freedom necessary to marry. Either there is already a pregnancy involved, or one or both of the parties were previously married, making it difficult or even impossible for them to receive the sacrament.

Mixed marriages, where one of the parties is not Catholic, and interfaith marriages, where one of the parties isn't even a baptized Christian, pose special challenges since the Catholic party is obliged to raise the children Catholic and the other party is often reluctant to do so. These marriages also present practical problems for the wedding liturgy itself, because it is not permissible for non-Catholics to receive Holy Communion. This restriction, when not properly understood, causes hard feelings between the families at the precise time when their unity should be accomplished and celebrated.

Wedding rehearsals are a constant irritant for priests who have to deal with large, unruly wedding parties, and people who aren't used to being in the church or aren't familiar with

Catholic worship. Bystanders become liturgical experts, infusing the liturgy with every sort of personal preference and creative innovation.

Wedding liturgies themselves become parties rather than prayer, making it nearly impossible to maintain any sense of decorum, any sense of the sacred. Guests arrive late, the bride goes into hiding, the groomsmen have been sitting in the church parking lot drinking, flower girls and ring bearers are very cute but too young to walk up the aisle without crying, the music is chosen from the "top forty list," and the photographer scrambles over the pews to direct the action rather than record it.

It's exceedingly difficult for the priest to stand in the pulpit with any degree of conviction and to speak about the permanence of marriage when guests are involved in their second or third marriage, about fidelity when spouses have been or will be unfaithful, about sanctity when the newlyweds process out of church never to be seen again, and about children when so many brides and grooms carry a contraceptive mentality into their marriage.

The secular mentality continues into the wedding reception, which nowadays is characterized by earsplitting music, too much drinking, vulgar language (even by the best man during the toast), and mandatory rituals that border on the pagan. Jesus and Mary, who graced the wedding feast at Cana, would surely be embarrassed by the festivities today!

Perhaps this list sounds depressing to you, but I assure you that such circumstances are not unusual. I've personally witnessed all of them, as have most priests. Is it any wonder that pastors find it easier and more satisfying to celebrate funerals rather than weddings?

The challenge of the Church today is to regain a sense of the sacred as we teach about marriage and celebrate weddings. It begins with clear and consistent catechesis about the nature and obligations of Holy Matrimony. The Church will certainly be countercultural in this matter, but our teaching will be a gift to our society.

And in planning and celebrating weddings, we need to return to practices that emphasize that marriage is a sacrament, not a social convenience, that a wedding is a prayer, not a parade.

What can couples do to prepare to receive the Sacrament of Holy Matrimony in a fitting way?

First, in dating and courtship, associate with people who are free to marry in the Catholic Church. So many fine young Catholics find themselves in a painful dilemma when they are forced to choose between marrying the one they love or maintaining their sacramental life in the Church. More often than not the Church loses. Remember also the advantage of marrying someone of your own faith—it brings about a more perfect union and eliminates many potential conflicts down the road.

Don't live together before marriage. It is an established fact that the divorce rate for couples who live together before marriage is much higher than for couples who don't. Cohabitation tarnishes your reputation, creates a nearly unavoidable occasion for sin, and causes scandal for others.

Live in chastity and purity, attend Mass on Sunday, receive the sacraments of the Church, and pray together. Your engagement is a beautiful time when God will be active in your life if you allow Him to do so, if you seek His grace and guidance.

Participate willingly in a marriage preparation program offered by the Church. It will help you and your intended spouse focus on essential elements of your future life together as you discuss faith, family, sexuality, children, communication, and finances.

In planning your wedding ceremony, resist social pressure and strive for simplicity. Remember, the larger and more grandiose your wedding, the more complications and tensions you'll encounter as the big day approaches. The essential requirements of your wedding are the two of you, your witnesses, the priest, and Jesus Christ. Be sure that the bridal party you've chosen is committed to celebrating your wedding in a spiritual and faith-filled way. Maintain a civil Christian atmosphere at your reception. You can still have the time of your life while avoiding pagan rituals and embarrassing moments.

Finally, in your married life be completely open to God's providence. You cannot begin to predict or control the future, but your faith in God and unconditional love for each other will be the pillars upon which you build your life together. Be receptive to the gift of children to complete your union, and remember that the number of children you have must include a consideration of God's will as well as your own.

There is so much at stake when we speak about Holy Matrimony. After all, healthy Christian marriages are the foundation of healthy families; and healthy families are the foundation of society. May we live to see the day when Holy Matrimony is once again holy, when it is celebrated and lived in a way that allows the love of God to shine through, illuminating the Church and the world.

Nurturing the Domestic Church

I always enjoy celebrating the Sacrament of Baptism, whether at the cathedral or in a local parish church. Baptism is such a beautiful sacrament, filled with spiritual significance, marked by the saving power and grace of Almighty God. Baptism is also a time of gratitude, pride, and joy for new parents as a child is welcomed into the family of the Church and begins a grace-filled friendship with the Lord Jesus Christ.

In presenting their child for Baptism, Catholic parents assume a serious responsibility to raise their child in the faith. This obligation of Catholic parenthood is clearly highlighted during the baptismal ceremony. At the beginning of the rite, the celebrant addresses the parents:

> You have asked to have your child baptized. In doing so you are accepting the responsibility of training him (her) in the practice of the faith. . . . Do you clearly understand what you are undertaking?

And the parents respond: "We are."

Again, later in the ceremony, as the parents and godparents are about to profess their faith and renew their own baptismal vows, the priest says to the parents:

> You must make it your constant care to bring your child up in the practice of the faith. . . . If your faith makes you ready to accept this responsibility, renew now the vows of your own Baptism. . . . This is the faith of the Church. This is the faith in which this child is about to be baptized.

As clear as this commitment seems to be, I wonder how many parents really understand the meaning of the promise they make to "train their children in the practice of the faith." In other words, we might ask, what are the obligations of being a Catholic parent?

Permit me to propose five obligations of a Catholic parent. While this list is not all inclusive, it does, I believe, touch upon many of the key areas.

(1) **Provide a Catholic education.** The Baptism rite challenges parents to be "the first teachers of their child in the ways of faith, the best of teachers." That statement underlines the fact that parents have the primary responsibility to instruct their children in the Catholic faith. That task of teaching takes place within the Church community, of course, and Catholic schools and catechetical programs play a very significant part in handing on the faith. But it is first of all parents who teach their children about God and the Church.

Some time ago, a man confronted me claiming that our religious education programs are woefully inadequate. He cited as an example his own daughter who had attended CCD for eight years and didn't know her basic prayers, the sacraments, commandments, and other important Catholic practices and traditions. I responded that our catechetical programs in the diocese are very sound, and that they do a good job in teaching the Catholic faith, especially in light of the very limited time children spend in religious education classrooms. The truth is, however, that if this man's daughter didn't know her Catholic prayers and practices, the sacraments and commandments, he needed to examine his own role as the primary teacher of his child in the ways of faith.

(2) **Ensure that children receive other sacraments.** Baptism is essential to the life of the Christian. It serves as the foundation

upon which the whole Christian life is based. It is, though, only the beginning. I like to think of Baptism as planting a seed of God's life within the soul of a child. But like every good seed, it needs to be carefully nourished if it is to grow and bear good fruit.

The divine life a child receives in Baptism is fulfilled by other sacraments, especially Confirmation and Eucharist, which complete the child's initiation into the Church and seal the friendship with Christ. Parents are responsible for preparing their children and leading them to receive the other sacraments. That's why parents are sometimes asked to be part of sacramental preparation programs, so that they can accompany their children as they grow in the life of faith.

It is also the duty of parents to see that their children attend Sunday Mass and receive Holy Communion and the Sacrament of Reconciliation on a regular basis. Parents need to be witnesses of the value of Catholic, sacramental marriages, especially in a time when so many other less desirable options are readily available to young people.

(3) **Be practicing Catholics.** From many conversations I've had with pastors, I know that nothing frustrates them more than parents who "dump their kids in Catholic school or CCD" and never attend Sunday Mass themselves. The failure to be practicing Catholics, especially with respect to Sunday Mass attendance, effectively contradicts everything children are taught in Catholic school or CCD.

How do children learn what it means to be an adult Catholic? By watching what their parents do! It is crucial that parents be practicing Catholics, for their own salvation and that of their children. That means attending Mass every Sunday and holy day, receiving Holy Communion, going to Confession regularly, taking an active part in the life of the Church, generously supporting the Church, and being obedient to the teachings and disciplines of the Church. Not all children who have the example of faithful parents will turn out to be practicing Catholics, but the chance that they will do so without the persuasive example of their parents is minimal.

(4) **Provide clear moral example.** In forming their moral conscience and attempting to live as moral people, children and youth face tremendous negative pressures—from their peers and from the popular culture around them. To effectively counteract the tidal wave of immorality to which their children are exposed, parents need to manifest a Christian life in which their faith in Christ is evident and consistent.

Children and youth watch carefully, and they can spot hypocrisy in a heartbeat. Parents, because they are role models, have an added duty to act morally, keep the commandments, and follow the teachings of Christ and His Church. Will children learn to be honest if they know that parents cheat on their income taxes? Will children learn to use alcohol responsibly if parents party and drink to excess? How will children learn to respect and obey their parents if Mom and Dad are always fighting?

(5) **Encourage vocations to the priesthood and religious life.** The work of fostering vocations to the priesthood and religious life belongs to the entire Catholic community, but parents have a unique and privileged role to play. Vocations to serve the Church are planted and nourished in the "domestic Church," the family. Too often, however, we encounter parents who are obstacles rather than allies in fostering Church vocations.

Parents have a very serious, God-given obligation to encourage their children to consider God's call to priesthood or religious life. To have a child devote his or her life to the service of God and the Church is not to "lose them" or "give them up," but is a noble and beautiful gift, a blessing for any Catholic family.

Now . . . that's quite a formidable list I've assembled here, quite a challenge for parents, and no doubt there are other responsibilities I've overlooked. But this is exactly what parents bargain for when they procreate children and present them for Baptism in the Church.

Perhaps it seems difficult, even impossible, to be good Catholic parents today, but parents need not be frightened or discouraged. If they faithfully accept their obligations and do their very best, they can be certain that God will be with them as they travel the demanding but rewarding road of Catholic parenthood.

Sacrifice: Something Precious for God

Recently I wrote a letter to the entire Church in the Diocese of Youngstown in which I described the growing shortage of priests and what that would mean for our priests and parishes. Specifically I wrote:

> It is inevitable that this declining number will have serious consequences for parish life and, also, for the priests themselves. . . . Everyone—priests, religious, and laity—will be asked to make some personal sacrifices to respond to the changing pastoral scene.

In response to my observations, one member of the diocese wrote a very sincere and thoughtful letter expressing her concern for the well-being of our priests. She suggested that we were creating an impossible "job description" for priests and I quote, in part, from her presentation:

> Wanted: Roman Catholic Priest. Administrator, counselor, mediator, preacher, educator, community activist, presider at liturgy. Excellent people skills are a must. Work 14-16 hours per day, live alone, low pay. Marriage not permitted. Must be willing to accept assignments that are not necessarily first preference. Must be willing to accept very large parishes or serve more than one parish. . . . Normal retirement age is 75, but will be asked to keep working beyond that age until gravely ill.

The letter writer went on to ask, and I paraphrase, "I worry about our pastor and other priests. How much can they do? Are they just supposed to work until they drop dead? What kind of Church are we?"

I must admit, I was very taken by the obvious sincerity and compassion of the lady who wrote to me, and I am quite sympathetic to her point of view. There's no question—we do ask an awful lot of our priests today. Priestly ministry is very demanding. Every day I thank God that the priests of this diocese respond as generously as they do.

But my personal reflection on this topic took me a step farther. My question is this: Do we really ask more of our priests today than in previous generations, or are the demands just somewhat different? Throughout the history of the Church, haven't many priests and religious had to sacrifice and suffer for Christ? Should our age be any different? And what did Jesus ask of His followers? If we put together a job description using the words of Jesus, it might look something like this:

"He instructed them to take nothing for the journey but a walking stick—no food, no sack, no money in their belts" (cf. Mk. 6:8).

"If any man would come after me, let him deny himself and take up his cross and follow me" (Mk. 8:34).

"[W]hoever would be great among you must be your servant, and whoever would be first among you must be slave of all" (Mk. 10:43-44).

"[T]ake heed to yourselves; for they will deliver you up to councils . . . and you will be hated by all for my name's sake" (Mk. 13:9, 13).

"Foxes have holes, and birds of the air have nests; but the Son of man has nowhere to lay his head. . . . No one who puts his hand to the plow and looks back is fit for the kingdom of God" (Lk. 9:58, 62).

"So therefore, whoever of you does not renounce all that he has cannot be my disciple" (Lk. 14:33).

"[W]hen you are old, you will stretch out your hands, and another will gird you and carry you where you do not wish to go" (Jn. 21:18).

Hey, Jesus . . . Hold on for just one darn minute! I'm worried about your apostles. How much can they do? Are they just supposed to work until they drop dead? What kind of Church do you have?

Do we ask more of our priests today than Jesus asked of His followers? I don't think so. Jesus didn't recruit wimps then, and He certainly doesn't recruit wimps today. Men who step forward to serve Christ and His Church must be strong, generous men, willing to sacrifice and suffer for Christ and His Church.

The generosity we find in our priests today is, it seems to me, characteristic of the followers of Christ in every age. Consider the great martyrs of the Church who bravely suffered physical pain and horrible deaths because of their beliefs. Think of the missionaries of the Church who, throughout history and still today, abandoned everything—family, friends, material comfort, and personal safety—to preach the Gospel to the ends of the earth. And don't forget the missionaries even in our own country who traveled alone into uncharted territory on horseback, all their possessions in a backpack, to establish the Church here.

It's true: Priests are required to work very hard, with long hours, and for many years for the sake of the Gospel. But in light of the commitment demanded by the Lord, and consistent with the noble and generous tradition that is ours, we can do no less.

My correspondent adds: "I will try to encourage young men to consider the priesthood . . . [but] I certainly wouldn't choose the priesthood as a career, with that type of (job) description." She is suggesting that young men won't be interested in the priesthood if it is too hard, or demanding. On the contrary, I am convinced that young people will respond to challenges, that they want work that is personally fulfilling. If prospective candidates for the priesthood are not willing to work long and hard for the kingdom of God, they need not apply.

An additional point. Sacrifice certainly isn't reserved only for those in "Church vocations"—priests and religious. We shouldn't overlook the substantial, sometimes even heroic sacrifices husbands and wives, mothers and fathers make in the living out of their vocations. Parents work hard, very hard, to fulfill their obligations and to provide suitable homes and necessities of life for their families. They are pulled in many directions: by their professional lives, by the Church and community, by the needs of their children. They have many concerns: the stability of their marriage, job security, the health of aging parents, the quality of the education their children receive, and the social and moral climate in which their children live.

Someone once observed that while consecrated religious take solemn vows of poverty, chastity, and obedience, married folk live those commitments too. They assume poverty, in that material possessions are never completely their own, but are at the disposal of all family members; chastity, in that they are required to be faithful to their spouse for life, despite the many opportunities and temptations they face; and obedience, in that they must always be mindful of and responsive to the will of their spouse and children, putting family needs ahead of their own.

This "job description" for husbands and wives, mothers and fathers is pretty formidable, isn't it? Many of the laity live truly sacrificial lives as they seek to fulfill their God-given vocations, day in, day out.

The dictionary defines sacrifice as "an act of offering something precious to God." Isn't that exactly what Jesus did in His suffering and death on the Cross? Isn't that exactly what He expects of us, regardless of our vocation in life?

Sacrifice, "offering something precious to God," is part and parcel of the Christian life. But it has particular meaning for priests and religious who have consecrated themselves to Christ. Without minimizing for one moment the reality of the sacrifices they make, let's keep in mind that for followers of Christ, there is no other way!

Ministry in the Church

The feast of the Baptism of the Lord, celebrated each year in January, is an invitation to reflect on the consequences of our own Baptism. As the Catechism summarizes for us:

> The fruit of Baptism, or baptismal grace, is a rich reality that includes forgiveness of original sin and all personal sins, birth into the new life by which man becomes an adoptive son of the Father, a member of Christ and a temple of the Holy Spirit. By this very fact the person baptized is incorporated into the Church, the Body of Christ, and made a sharer in the priesthood of Christ (no. 1279).

Christ calls all members of the Church to share in His priesthood, which entails lifelong service to the Church and the world. While this concept of ecclesial ministry is rooted in the Scriptures and formed by the traditional teaching of the Church, it has certainly received new emphasis since the Second Vatican Council. In fact, it seems that the tremendous increase in the number of people actively involved in the mission of the Church is one of the council's most positive and long-lasting outcomes.

While a variety of Church documents make some reference to ministry in the Church, the most recent is a 1997 Vatican document entitled *Instruction on Certain Questions Regarding the Collaboration of Non-ordained Faithful in the Sacred Ministry of the Priest.* This document is important not only because of the topic it addresses, but also because of its form. It is unique in that it is a cooperative effort of eight different offices of the Vatican and personally approved *in forma specifica* by the pope. While the instruction makes a number of particular applications to contemporary issues, two general principles should be highlighted.

First, it emphasizes that all the baptized are to share in the work of the Church, and that this role is essential:

> The source of the call addressed to all members of the Mystical Body to participate actively in the mission and edification of the People of God is to be found in the mystery of the Church. . . . The Church cannot put aside this task because it is part of her very nature, as the People of God, and also because she has need of it in order to realize her own mission of evangelization.

The document also clarifies another very significant point. While all the members of the Church are called to mission, there is an important distinction between the ministry of the ordained and that of the non-ordained. The clarity of this distinction is essential if both vocations in the Church are to prosper:

> The Second Vatican Ecumenical Council refers particularly to this when it teaches: "The hierarchy entrusts the laity with certain charges more closely connected with the duties of pastors: in the teaching of Christian doctrine, for example, in certain liturgical actions in the care of souls" (Decree on the Apostolate of the Laity).
>
> Since these tasks are more closely linked to the duties of pastors (which office requires reception of the sacrament of Orders), it is necessary that all who are in any way involved in this collaboration exercise particular care to safeguard the nature and mission of sacred ministry and the vocation and secular character of the lay faithful. It must be remembered that "collaboration with" does not in fact mean "substitution for."

With these two fundamental principles as our context, then, allow me to suggest four points that are important to any discussion of ministry in the Church today.

The first is that all ministry is an extension of the work of Jesus the Good Shepherd. And what does it mean to be a shepherd in the Church? It means, quite simply, to teach, to serve, and to sanctify God's people for the sake of the salvation of souls. These perennial tasks apply to any shepherd in the Church: Jesus Himself, the pope, bishops, or priests. Every ministry of the Church is derived in some fashion from one of these functions—teaching, serving, and sanctifying.

The second point is that ministry doesn't exist primarily for the sake of the minister, but for the good of the Church. The First Letter to the Corinthians, chapter 12, teaches that while there are many different gifts, they are all given by the same Spirit and intended to build up the Body of Christ. This means, then, that no person can claim as a personal "right" any particular ministry. Further, all ministries are supervised by leaders of the Church—by the bishop in a diocese, by the pastor in a parish—whose duty it is to discern the needs of the community.

It should also be mentioned here that not every service in the Church is a "ministry." Baking cookies, helping to park cars, or calling bingo numbers may be and often are valuable services given out of generosity and love, but can hardly be called "ministries" in the strict sense of the term. If "ministry" refers to everything, it means nothing.

Third, there is a complementarity among the members of the Church as related to ministry. Saint Paul reminds us that the body needs many different parts, each performing a distinct but important function. One part of the body should not feel inferior to or be threatened by another. A foot cannot say, "Because I am not a hand, I do not belong to the body" (1 Cor. 12:15).

Recent synods of bishops have systematically addressed the specific contributions of various vocations in the Church. It is the primary work of the ordained clergy to minister to God's people in word and sacrament. It is the primary work of consecrated religious to bear witness to Christ by a faithful living out of their vows. And it is the primary work of the laity to change the world, instilling Christian values by participating in secular affairs. Such distinctions recognize that there is some legitimate overlapping that occurs in these roles. But nonetheless these are important distinctions that are sometimes blurred in the recent experience of the Church.

The fourth point is that the foundation of every ministry in the Church involves a radical and personal discipleship of Jesus Christ. Every minister must have as his or her first priority a desire to grow in holiness. This is everyone's vocation. The path to holiness is clear: reception of the sacraments, personal prayer, immersion in the Word of God, keeping the commandments, ongoing formation, and the exercise of charity and justice in everyday life. It should be obvious that only by first knowing and loving Jesus can anyone claim to be His authentic witness in the exercise of any ministry.

In their active ministry the laity are clearly fulfilling the promise of their Baptism, and how necessary that is for the Church and the world today. As the pope reminds us in his recent letter, *Ecclesia in America*, "The renewal of the Church in America will not be possible without the active presence of the laity. Therefore, they are largely responsible for the future of the Church" (no. 44).

Playing God in the New Millennium

> *Man has made stupendous progress in the domination and rational organization of the forces of nature, such that he tends to extend this domination to his own total being . . . even to the laws which regulate the transmission of life. . . . This new state of things gives rise to new questions.*
> —Pope Paul VI, *Humanae Vitae* (1968), nos. 2-3

This prophecy contained in *Humanae Vitae* has been fulfilled. In 1997, for example, *USA Today* reported on the birth of a baby girl to a sixty-three-year-old woman, and posed some of the more practical questions surrounding this bizarre event. Does an older woman have the energy to raise a child? (When she is sixty-five, this woman will be chasing a two-year-old. She'll be in her seventies when teenage rebellion strikes.) How available will she be to that child over the course of twenty or thirty years? Will an older woman live long enough to raise her child?

There are more profound moral issues at stake as well, issues that need to be addressed in this and similar scenarios we face in the world today. What does the Church have to say about all this? What are the principles that guide our moral judgments as we evaluate the impact of such scientific advances?

Well, for starters, as much as it has been misunderstood and maligned, the encyclical of Pope Paul VI on the transmission of human life, *Humanae Vitae*, was right, prophetically right! Our domination of the forces of nature does give rise to new and perplexing questions. And as the encyclical predicted, this human intervention in the natural order has led to real chaos in segments of society where human experimentations are taking place today.

The area of medical ethics, especially in human life issues, is a moral minefield. Think of some of the practices of our day: in vitro fertilization, embryo experimentation, genetic engineering, cloning, embryonic stem cell research, surrogate parenting, and assisted suicide. In these procedures we are not only "extending domination over our total being," but we are also treading on sacred ground, delving into areas that belong primarily to God.

As we venture then into this realm where the fantasies of science fiction become the realities of everyday life, we need to be mindful of a number of essential moral parameters.

The first principle is the following: the fact that something *can* be done does not mean that it *should* be done. As human science evolves, there must be moral limitations. Responsibility is the chaperone of scientific progress. The world was reminded of this rule, for example, in the development of biological, chemical, and nuclear weapons. While we learned how to make them, we also realized that we dare not use them. Treaties have been developed to limit or eliminate their use.

The same applies to medical, biological inventions. The fact that we learn to do something with human life does not automatically justify its use. Every new technology and procedure must be examined in light of God's unchanging moral law.

Another teaching of our faith is that our will is always subject to God's will. Man has been endowed with intelligence and freedom, and it is possible for us to do our will rather than God's will—but that's what we call sin! Our faith in God, Creator and Judge, leads us to seek and do God's will even when that leads to personal disappointment or sacrifice.

In other words, merely wanting a child does not justify the use of illicit medical means to produce a child, even for loving, properly motivated parents in a stable marriage. "Thy will be done," Jesus taught us to pray. "Not my will, but thine, be done." Jesus Himself prayed in Gethsemane. "Let it be done to me according to your word," Mary responded at the moment of the Annunciation. The hallmark of a holy person is the desire to know and do God's will in every circumstance of life.

Yet another important factor in judging medical procedures related to human life is the need to respect the natural law, that "light of understanding infused in us by God whereby we understand what must be done and what must be avoided" (Pope John Paul II, *Veritatis Splendor*, no. 40). Paul VI emphasized the proper role of the Church in teaching the principles that derive from natural law, which are also "necessary for salvation" (*Humanae Vitae*, no. 4). And more recently, the Catechism teaches: "The natural law, the Creator's very good work, provides the solid foundation on which man can build the structure of moral rules to guide his choices" (no. 1959).

In short, in making decisions about procreation and other human life issues, we are obliged to follow the natural law, which is revealed by God and explained by the Church. In the natural law we always discover the will of God.

And when we think about the creation of children, we need to recall the fundamental purposes of marriage and human sexuality as given us by God, for it is only within the sacred confines of marriage that human life may be licitly created. The twofold purpose of marriage is to give life and to give love. "God who created man out of love also calls him to love. . . . And this love which God blesses is intended to be fruitful" (Catechism, no. 1604).

Giving life and giving love—these are the two essential purposes of Holy Matrimony and human sexuality. For a couple to enter into marriage without the intention of having children is to enter a sterile and incomplete union. And to create human life, whether in a union outside marriage or in a laboratory test tube, without the solidarity of human love in Holy Matrimony is contrary to the will of God, regardless of how "fulfilled" it makes someone feel.

One needs only to read the headlines or watch the TV talk shows to see the havoc that results when biological life-giving is separated from holy love-giving in marriage, through surrogacy or test-tube fertilization. How often stable family life is left in ruins, presented as a curious relic of the past, rather than the ideal of human society. People who undertake these abnormal procedures do so to satisfy their own wants, ignorant of the needs of others, especially the children born of such deeds. How often already have we heard of lawsuits in which the parents contend the "ownership" of children born of laboratory procedures or prearranged unions?

The *USA Today* article asked the question, "Who is to say that a [sixty-three-year-old] woman cannot have a child?" The answer, of course, is that God says that a sixty-three-year-old cannot have a child. That's why the female biological clock, that clock set by the Creator Himself, the clock that enables women to bear children, ceases ticking long before she is sixty-three. To play with that timeline is absurd, pretentious, and ultimately unfair to others.

In the garden of paradise, Adam and Eve ate the forbidden fruit because they wanted to be like God. In the end, they lost the paradise that had been given them.

Later the people of Babel, moved by pride in their own achievements, said, "Come, let us build ourselves a city, and a tower with its top in the heavens, and let us make a name for ourselves" (Gen. 11:4). God was displeased and said, "[N]othing that they propose to do will now be impossible for them" (Gen. 11:6). And God destroyed their tower, and the people were thrown into chaos.

In thinking about in vitro fertilization such as that which produced a baby in the body of a sixty-three-year-old woman, we do well to keep in mind the biblical example of Adam and Eve as well as the people of Babel. Every time mankind tries to play God, we get ourselves into serious trouble.

As an advanced, sophisticated, and highly technological society, we need to have more respect for the natural law, God's law, than ever before. Not everything that *can* be done *should* be done. That's an important truth to remember as we advance into the brave, if sometimes foolish, new world!

Unconditionally Pro-Life

This situation, with its lights and shadows, ought to make us all fully aware that we are facing an enormous and dramatic clash between good and evil, death and life, the "culture of death" and the "culture of life." We find ourselves not only "faced with" but necessarily "in the midst of" this conflict: we are all involved and we share in it, with the inescapable responsibility of choosing to be unconditionally pro-life.

—Pope John Paul II
Evangelium Vitae (The Gospel of Life)
no. 28, original emphasis

In his historical 1995 encyclical, *Evangelium Vitae* (EV), our Holy Father characterizes our society as a "culture of death." He speaks of widespread moral uncertainty, a "structure of sin," and a "war of the powerful against the weak." He writes that this reality in many cases takes the form of a veritable "culture of death," which is actively fostered by powerful cultural, economic, and political currents.

In the face of this pervasive culture of death, it is the obligation of the Church and individual Christians to speak insistently and courageously about the sanctity of human life. No exceptions allowed.

The moral fabric of our society is being challenged every day by a triple threat against the sanctity of human life, diverse in its circumstances, but similar in its effect of eroding our respect for human life: abortion, euthanasia, and capital punishment.

Abortion continues to be the great moral pestilence of our time. How can any nation that allows and sometimes even pays for the routine killing of its babies expect that there will not be a lessening of respect for other persons, disintegration of our families, schools, and neighborhoods, and violence in our streets?

Partial birth abortion is especially repugnant, for in this case a baby is killed even after it is viable, even as it is about to be born. Even Congress itself defines the procedure as "an abortion in which the person performing the abortion partially vaginally delivers a living fetus before killing the fetus and completing the delivery." It is simply unbelievable that our nation, because of the strident lobbying of just a few extremists, continues to allow this horrible practice.

The arguments for "reproductive freedom" and the so-called "right to choose" are tiresome and trivial in light of the real problems we face. Keep in mind that every time an abortion takes place, regardless of the circumstances, a life is ended and a baby dies. And the foundation of our society continues to crumble.

By the way, why is it that the secular media insist on calling those who promote life "anti-abortionists" or "anti-choice" when they prefer to be called "pro-life"? Don't the "pro-lifers" deserve the same deference from the media that other special interest groups and minorities receive, and rightfully so?

The second prong of the triple threat to life is assisted suicide, a practice that preys upon the vulnerability of good people during the troubled times of their lives. Pain and suffering are an inevitable part of human existence, and from the point of view of our faith, can even be redemptive. As difficult as circumstances might be, however,

> [t]o concur with the intention of another person to commit suicide and to help in carrying it out through so-called "assisted suicide" means to cooperate in, and at times to be the actual perpetrator of, an injustice which can never be excused, even if it is requested (EV 66).

We need to be alert to the growing acceptance of assisted suicide in our culture and oppose it vigorously. The Church is most clear in teaching that "euthanasia is a grave violation of the law of God since it is the deliberate and morally unacceptable killing of a human person" (EV 65).

Finally, one of the real challenges for pro-lifers in the United States will be to counter the growing support for the death penalty. Without a doubt, this issue is in a far different category from the other human life issues already mentioned, and the Church recognizes it as such. Many of those in favor of capital punishment are well motivated and are, in fact, trying to protect human life from the evil of violent crime in our country.

The problem with some of those who favor the death penalty, however, is that they seek vengeance rather than justice. You've seen the news reports from outside of a prison on the eve of the execution. "Let him burn," the crowd chants. (In former times this was translated, "Crucify Him, crucify Him!") "I'll volunteer to throw the switch myself," another adds, much too eagerly. When people voice these vengeful feelings, their spirits die as surely as the body of the one being executed.

In *Evangelium Vitae*, the Holy Father affirms that if bloodless means are sufficient to defend human lives against the aggressor and to protect the public order and the safety of persons, public authority must limit itself to such means. Referring to cases in which the death penalty would be justified, the pope says, "today, however, . . . such cases are very rare, if not practically non-existent" (cf. Catechism, no. 2267).

I, too, recoil in horror and disgust against some of the crimes I read about or hear about in the news. We wonder how one human being could ever commit these heinous and senseless crimes against another. It is precisely in these cases, however, that we have the opportunity to make the most compelling statement in favor of human life, by saying that even the life of the worst criminal has intrinsic value. Putting a person to death does nothing to foster our respect for life, but is, in fact, another step down the slippery slope to the bottomless pit of the culture of death.

We could mention many other issues that threaten the dignity of human life today, including: the abuse of drugs and alcohol that ruins so many individuals and families; domestic and neighborhood violence that causes pain, suffering and death; and the unjust treatment of immigrants, refugees, and migrant workers who come to our country.

In the context of this "culture of death," it is easy to get discouraged, to believe that there is nothing we can do about the violent world in which we live. And yet we hear the persistent call of Jesus to be the "salt of the earth" and the "light of the world." We hear the challenge of the pope: "We need to bring the *Gospel of life* to the heart of every man and woman and to make it penetrate every part of society" (EV 80, original emphasis).

In practical terms, how do we "bring the Gospel of life to the heart of every man and woman?" How do we accomplish this lofty goal?

First, of course, we pray with persistence and faith. We seek God's power to support us in the battle for human life in our day. We ask God to enlighten the minds, change the hearts, and forgive the sins of those who undermine the sanctity of human life. And we ask God to help and bless all those who are victims of the culture of death that surrounds us. I am convinced that ultimately the battle for human life will be won not in our courtrooms, legislative halls, or medical laboratories, but in the sanctuary of the human heart, an arena to which only God has access.

Second, we commit ourselves to a course of personal action in support of the pro-life cause. We can read to be well informed of the issues. We can write letters to legislators and newspapers seeking to form proper public opinion. We can offer financial support to pro-life organizations and participate in their programs and activities.

It is particularly important to emphasize that we can—and should—vote for candidates who are publicly committed to defending and promoting human life. As the pope teaches, "This task is the particular responsibility of *civil leaders.* Called to serve the people and the common good, they have a duty to make courageous choices in support of life. . . . [N]o one can ever renounce this responsibility" (EV 90, original emphasis).

And finally, we should examine carefully our own attitudes and behaviors to be certain that they are consistent with the message we proclaim and the Gospel we preach. Are our thoughts, words, and deeds truly expressive of our commitment to life?

> [T]he *Gospel of life* is to be celebrated above all in *daily living,* which should be filled with self-giving love for others. In this way, our lives will become a genuine and responsible acceptance of the gift of life and a heartfelt song of praise and gratitude to God who has given us this gift (EV 86, original emphasis).

But to return to the issue of abortion. Someday, you know, you will stand before the judgment seat of Almighty God and make a full account of your life here on earth. At that moment, which position would you rather defend: that you supported, encouraged, or even allowed, by your silence, the death of innocent children in abortion? Or that you did your very best, made every possible effort, to defend and protect the innocent life God Himself created? I don't know about you, but for me the choice is crystal clear!

O Mary, bright dawn of the new world, Mother of the living, to you we entrust the cause of life. . . . Grant that all who believe in your Son may proclaim the Gospel of life with honesty and love to the people of our time.

The Death Penalty: WWJD?

[H]e stood up and said to them, "Let him who is without sin among you be the first to throw a stone at her."... Jesus looked up and said to her, "Woman, where are they? Has no one condemned you?" She said, "No one, Lord." And Jesus said, "Neither do I condemn you."

—Jn. 8:7, 10-11

In the context of the solemn observance of Good Friday and the death of Jesus on the Cross, I encourage you to evaluate carefully your attitude about the death penalty.

In asking you to do so, I recognize fully that this is a very difficult, even emotional issue. Despite the evolving clarity of the Church's teaching on the subject, many people, including many faithful Catholics, are troubled by this issue. Even some "pro-lifers," staunch opponents of abortion and euthanasia, draw the line at this point. Nonetheless, the teaching of the Church and, more pointedly, the example of Christ Himself, cannot be avoided.

The reasons people use to support the death penalty in our country are understandable. Some crimes are terribly violent and cruel, and the criminals who perpetrate them deserve the most severe punishment. The desire to execute criminals can also arise from the positive motive of seeking justice and promoting the common good, and the fear that anything less than death will encourage crime and violence in our society. And it has been argued that the death penalty is important for victims and their families, to bring about some measure of personal satisfaction and closure to their ordeal.

While all these arguments would appear to have some merit, they are countered by other relevant facts and by fundamental moral values that are central to the teachings of Christ and His Church.

We need to acknowledge that the teaching of the Church on this issue has developed in recent years. While maintaining always the dignity of every human life, the Church has historically affirmed the legitimate right of government to protect society and promote the common good by punishing wrongdoers, even by executing the offender if no other means of securing justice were possible.

But conditions in society have changed, and it is clear that the circumstances that allowed the use of the death penalty no longer exist. The teaching of the Church against capital punishment has become much more explicit. The *Catechism of the Catholic Church* and Pope John Paul II's landmark encyclical, *Evangelium Vitae* (The Gospel of Life), have strengthened the Church's position. And during his historic visit to St. Louis in 1999, the pope issued a passionate plea:

> The new evangelization calls for followers of Christ who are unconditionally pro-life: who will proclaim, celebrate, and serve the Gospel of life in every situation. . . . I renew the appeal I made for a consensus to end the death penalty, which is both cruel and unnecessary.

From a practical perspective, we know there are many serious defects in the administration of the death penalty that render it unjust. First, it is well documented that the application of the death penalty in the United States has racial overtones, and that a disproportionate number of those on death row are minorities or poor. In other words, if you are wealthy and white, and can afford first-class lawyers, you have a much better chance than others of avoiding the death penalty, even if you have committed the same crime.

We know, too, that in exercising the death penalty, mistakes can be made, putting innocent people to death. Recently, Governor George Ryan of Illinois placed a moratorium on the death penalty in his state when it was discovered that over the past two decades Illinois freed thirteen inmates from death row because of demonstrated errors in their convictions or the judicial process. In most cases, prosecutors were forced to admit they had the wrong man after they were confronted with new DNA evidence, new witnesses, or confessions from others. Similar results have been found in other studies across the nation.

On another point, it is sometimes argued that the death penalty is needed to bring about justice and a sense of closure to the families of murder victims. More often than not, that's simply not true. One therapist who works extensively with families of victims has said, "Taking a life doesn't fill the void (victims experience), but it's generally not until after the execution that families realize this." And in a recent statement about the death penalty, the bishops of Pennsylvania insisted that survivors' well-being can not be rooted in vengeance: "True emotional, spiritual, and even physical healing is found in the compassionate embrace of Jesus who practices forgiveness and teaches us to do the same."

At this point it is important to note that opposition to capital punishment should not be construed as complacency toward crime or a lack of concern for the victims of crime. The Church and the entire community have a serious obligation to lend support and comfort to victims of crime and their families so that the healing of Jesus of which the bishops write can become a reality.

When all is said and done, the use of the death penalty, rather than promoting the common good, demeans us all. Again, the bishops of Pennsylvania:

Reliance on the use of the death penalty creates a greater harm to society by reinforcing the idea that violence is a solution to society's problems. The death penalty will not overcome violent crime any more than abortion will end the problem of unwanted pregnancy or euthanasia will solve the problem of aging and illness.

And in their recent statement on the criminal justice system, *Responsibility, Rehabilitation and Restoration: A Catholic Perspective on Crime and Criminal Justice,* the U.S. bishops conclude:

We wish to renew our call for an end to capital punishment. Capital punishment is cruel, unnecessary, and arbitrary. It fails to live up to our deep conviction that all human life is sacred. . . . But most of all, we are asking whether we can teach that killing is wrong by killing those who have been convicted of killing others.

Across the land, the debate over the use of capital punishment will continue, and sometimes the rhetoric itself will be violent and vengeful, even frightening. As disciples of Christ, however, we need to rise above the political, sociological, and economic arguments to consider the example of Jesus Christ.

In so doing we recall that Jesus Himself was the innocent victim of a cruel death sentence. That fact in itself should give us something to think about.

But beyond that, in evaluating the morality of the death penalty, as in every other situation of life, it is important to ask WWJD—What would Jesus do? Or even better, because we have a clear example in the Gospel, What *did* Jesus do?

In the single instance when Jesus confronted the use of the death penalty, that is, in the story of the woman caught in adultery, about to be stoned to death, His intervention and words led to her release from execution. Jesus rejected the use of capital punishment, even though it was required by the laws and circumstances of His time and place. That's what Jesus did, and no doubt would do today, regarding the death penalty!

My own state of Ohio has reinstituted the death penalty. How sad, how unnecessary. Ohio would be far better off to avoid this violent and counterproductive road. It would be much better to institute a moratorium on the death penalty in this state at least until all the circumstances, consequences, and alternatives can be carefully studied.

In the meantime, in addressing this issue, members of the Church and all followers of Jesus Christ should carefully and prayerfully consider the example and words of Jesus. The time has come to end the death penalty, create a more civilized and noble society, and insist once again on the unconditional sanctity of human life.

IV

Praying with the Church

Have You Prayed about It?

Every family has a few special heirlooms, special not because they're worth much money, but because of their meaning in the life of a family.

In my family's home in Pittsburgh, we had a little, homemade, plaster of paris plaque with a brown background and yellow lettering that read, "Have you prayed about it?" My Dad in particular made frequent reference to that saying. Anytime there was a family decision to be made or problem to be solved, he asked simply, "Have you prayed about it?"

That plaque disappeared from our home—I suspect that my sister pilfered it for use in her own home with her own family. But that question has come back to me time and time again.

Have you prayed about it? The lesson contained in those five simple words is clear and timeless, a reminder of the importance and power of prayer in our daily lives. Prayer is the Internet of the spiritual life. It lifts up our hearts and minds to the Lord and places us in contact with the living God. Prayer doesn't change the heart or mind of God. God already knows what we need long before we ask, and His love for us is much greater than we can ever imagine. It's rather presumptuous to think that we could tell God something He doesn't already know, or move Him to a love He doesn't already possess.

But prayer changes *us*. It opens us up to God's presence and power. It is an act of faith that draws upon God's grace, an act of trust that allows us to rest in the hands of God. We pray knowing that whatever happens, God will still be with us, loving us, and taking care of us.

Have you prayed about it? The "it" is not identified on the plaque, and I'm quite sure that's by design. The "it" about which we should pray is anything and everything that is part of our journey in life.

Naturally we turn to prayer first of all when we are in trouble, when we face a serious problem in life: the loss of a job, medical emergency, a child gone astray, a failing marriage. These sad events are all part of human experience, and most often they can't be solved by human devices alone. In confronting these challenges we need to ask, "Have we prayed about it?" Have we asked for God's guidance and peace, confident that with God all things are possible?

We should pray about "it" when "it" involves an important decision in our lives. I think especially of the young people at critical crossroads in their lives, those graduating from high school or college contemplating the promise of the future. Other people also have major decisions to make, decisions about their education, vocation, and relationships. Remember that God is the ultimate source of wisdom and truth. We should never try to make decisions all by ourselves, but always with God, in prayer.

"It" can be our struggle with a serious moral question. We try really hard to be good and to do good, but often we find ourselves in situations rife with temptation. In those moments, that snake Satan slithers into our lives and lures us away from our primary commitments. He tempts us to do what is easy and pleasurable instead of that which is good and holy. In the midst of such temptation, we need God's grace in our lives. We should urgently pray about it, for the salvation of our souls hangs in the balance.

Have you prayed about it? It is important to pray whenever we have failed and sinned, when we find ourselves separated from God and others. Sometimes our failures are so abysmal, so discouraging, that there's no hope for us, no way out. Or at least that's the way it seems. In these moments, in our prayer from the emptiness of our humanity, we encounter a gentle Father who loves us, embraces us, and want us to be with Him forever.

But our prayer isn't for bad times only. Prayer can celebrate our victories as well, the joyful, thankful moments: the birth of a child, a well-deserved promotion, the prospect of a restful vacation, a wedding anniversary, a successful surgery. So often we take these gifts for granted. But once in a while we have the good sense to remember the Source of all blessings, and like the thoughtful, thankful leper of the Gospel, we hasten back to the Lord to give Him thanks and praise.

Our prayer also serves to carry us beyond the limitations of our own life, keeping us mindful of other people, their sorrows and joys. Prayer sensitizes us to others who are not as blessed as we—the homeless and hungry of our neighborhoods; those who wrestle every day with abuse or addiction; those in our world who lack the very basic necessities of life such as clean drinking water, food, medicine, clothing, and secure shelter. Pray about it! God will help us to break down the selfish walls that surround us, isolating us from others. He will expand our narrow vision and break open our hearts so that we can better love our brothers and sisters in need.

Our prayer, for these intentions and others, can take many forms: the formal liturgy of the Church, personal time in the presence of Jesus in the Blessed Sacrament, a family Rosary, the excitement of a ballpark, or the quiet anxiety of a hospital waiting room. We can pray anywhere because God is already there, ready to listen and speak.

In our daily prayer we should turn to the saints, for they are really concerned about us and how we are doing; they are part of our spiritual family. And let's not forget that our primary helper in prayer is our Blessed Mother. Mary offers a sympathetic ear because in her own life she experienced so much. She is a powerful ally in prayer because she is close to God. Thus we might amend our question to ask, "Have you prayed to *her* about it?"

In the simplicity of his words and the example of his deeds, my Dad taught me many important lessons, but none more useful than the power of prayer. Thanks, Dad, for asking the question that is more helpful than all the answers in the world—"Have you prayed about it?"

So the Mass Is Ended—What's Next?

Perhaps you've heard the story of the priest who was assigned to offer early morning Mass every day for a group of nuns in a local convent. Each day after Mass the priest would stay at the convent to have breakfast with the sisters. One day at the conclusion of Mass, the priest announced, "Sisters, because of a change in my schedule, it will not be possible for me to have breakfast with you today." At which one of the elderly, hard-of-hearing nuns dutifully responded, "Thanks be to God!"

Of course in a more typical dismissal, the priest or deacon says, "The Mass is ended, go in peace to love and serve the Lord." These few words reveal an important theological truth and premise of our faith, namely, that there is a close connection between the liturgy we celebrate and the life we lead. The dismissal isn't simply an invitation to go home, but a commission—to "go in peace to love and serve the Lord."

It's true that we come to church on Sundays to find a spiritual oasis, a sanctuary of comfort, quiet, and peace in the midst of our turbulent, noisy world. (That's one of the reasons, by the way, I think it's so important to have some measure of silence in our churches rather than the cacophony we so often find today. After all, who really needs any more talk, any more noise in their lives?)

At the same time, however, the Christian commitment doesn't end with the conclusion of Mass; it only begins there.

---

* This chapter was first published in the September/October 2000 issue of *Be* magazine.

I've often thought that the real test of Christianity isn't in the church; anyone can be Christian in the church building. The real test of our faith is in the parking lot *after* Mass! It's there that our patience is tried as we jockey to get out of the lot first. It's there that we discover what it means to love our neighbor as ourselves!

In very clear terms, if our Catholic faith is to have any real meaning, the liturgy has to be more than an isolated event in the course of our week. The Mass we attend on Sunday should become our primary motivation and source of strength to live as disciples of Jesus Christ throughout the week.

In *Dies Domini*, his wonderful apostolic letter on keeping the Lord's Day holy, Pope John Paul II wrote the following:

> For the faithful who have understood the meaning of what they have done, the Eucharistic celebration does not stop at the church door. Like the first witnesses of the Resurrection, Christians who gather each Sunday to experience and proclaim the presence of the Risen Lord are called *to evangelize and bear witness* in their daily lives. . . . Once the assembly disperses, Christ's disciples return to their everyday surroundings with the commitment to make their whole life a gift, a spiritual sacrifice pleasing to God (no. 45, original emphasis).

The pope emphasizes that "the Eucharistic celebration does not stop at the church door." But more precisely, what is the connection between the liturgy we celebrate and the life we lead? How does participation in Sunday Mass affect my life throughout the week? While there are many answers to that question, permit me to suggest the following:

(1) **Our participation in Sunday Mass allows us to know the friendship and support of the Christian community in our daily lives.** It is at the Sunday Mass, more than any other parish event of the week, that the Church comes together in

faith and prayer. Many bonds of friendship are forged at that regular gathering. The Christian community formed at Sunday Mass travels with us every day, sharing our hopes and dreams, our victories and defeats, our suffering and our sorrow, assuring us that as members of the Body of Christ, we are never really alone in this world.

(2) The Sunday liturgy helps us to become more aware of God's presence in our daily lives. The Church teaches that Christ is really present in several diverse ways when the liturgy is celebrated—in the Word proclaimed, in the person of the priest, in the assembly of the faithful, and most of all, in the Sacrament of the Eucharist. At Sunday Mass we are surrounded by, saturated with, the presence of God. But that divine presence doesn't end when we return to the world. God remains with us throughout the week, and a faithful, conscious celebration of the Mass will make us inevitably more sensitive to that important reality.

(3) Participation in Sunday Mass lends us the moral strength we need to live as Christians. The Christian life is extremely demanding and, in the midst of a secular, materialistic, and atheistic world, can be nearly impossible, especially if we think we are all alone in our beliefs. Through the proclamation of the Word of God, the affirmation of a community that shares our beliefs and values, and the spiritual power of the Holy Eucharist, the Sunday Mass gives us the resolve, the moral courage we need to accept the challenges of the Gospel and to live our faith even in the most difficult of times and temptations.

(4) The Sunday Mass makes us more accepting of Church teaching. Some of the teachings of the Catholic Church—such as the sanctity of human life, the permanence of Holy

Matrimony, the reservation of Holy Orders to men alone, the need to forgive our enemies, and the call to build a just society—can be extremely difficult to understand and accept without a clear vision of faith. Participation in Sunday Mass helps us to appreciate the universal and divine nature of the Church, keeps us well informed, and encourages us to understand and accept even the most challenging of Church teachings with a docile and humble spirit.

(5) Participation in Sunday Mass inspires us to become more aware of and responsive to the needs of others. The Eucharist is to be loved; it is also to be lived. The presence of Christ in the Eucharist, worshipped and received, leads us to discover the presence of Christ in our brothers and sisters, particularly those who are poor and in need. Pope John Paul has written about this dimension of the Eucharist: "Closeness to Christ in silence and contemplation does not distance us from our contemporaries but, on the contrary, makes us more attentive and open to human joy and distress."[1] And recall what Saint John the Apostle has written: "[H]e who does not love his brother whom he has seen, cannot love God whom he has not seen" (1 Jn. 4:20).

(6) The Eucharistic celebration helps us to be more faithful in the living-out of our given vocation. We believe that each person is created for some particular task on earth. More than just a job or even a profession, the work we do in and through Christ is a true vocation—something for which God has created us and to which He has called us. Participation in the Sunday liturgy opens us to the will of God, making us more aware of what God is asking us to do. It also gives us the

---

[1] Letter on the 750th Anniversary of the Feast of Corpus Christi (May 28, 1996), no. 5.

courage we need to respond to His call and the perseverance necessary to be faithful—as priests, consecrated religious, or married persons, as baptized Christians.

(7) **The Sunday liturgy makes us more aware of our eternal destiny.** How easy it is to become earthbound, to get completely wrapped up in the details and drudgery of daily life. Once in a while we need to gaze beyond the horizon, to recall that our time on earth is meant to be temporary, that our final destiny is heaven. The Eucharist, as the foretaste of the heavenly banquet, lifts our hearts and minds beyond this life so that we may live responsibly here and now, maintaining a healthy perspective on the events of everyday life.

You see how many blessings and graces arise from the celebration of Sunday Mass. It is truly the source and summit of everything we are and all that we do as faith-filled Christians.

In short, the Mass should be for us a moment of profound transfiguration. In the Sunday Eucharist we experience the presence of the Risen Christ and, transfigured by what we have heard, seen, and received, we return to the world as faithful disciples and apostles, transforming the world into the kingdom of God.

Sunday Mass: What People Want

During vacation last summer I followed my normal practice of attending Sunday Mass as a "private citizen," that is, in secular attire, with the congregation, in the pews. Even though I truly cherish the privilege of leading the liturgy as I do almost every Sunday, it is also refreshing once in awhile to be on the other side of the altar. Doing so allows me to avoid the public spotlight, eliminates the pressure of having to prepare a homily, and helps me to return to the ministry relaxed and ready to go.

Whenever I join the rank and file, it's amazing how quickly I assume the characteristics of what might be considered the "typical Catholic." I planned my schedule so I wouldn't arrive at church too early. I sat toward the back of the church to avoid special involvement. I complained, at least mentally, about the length of the sermon. I was dismayed to learn that there would be a second collection—and yes, I did pry open my wallet to contribute to both! And I was appropriately irritated by the logjam of traffic in the parking lot after Mass.

Forget my need for "full, conscious, and active participation." I was on vacation. I wanted something short, sweet, and to the point, just enough to fulfill my Sunday obligation.

These bad habits aside, there were also some more beneficial lessons to be had from sitting in the pews. Doing so created a broader perspective for me and a renewed appreciation for the truly "faithful" who come to Mass Sunday after Sunday. It gave me the opportunity to reflect on the nature of the Church and the function of the liturgy.

As I sat in the Florida church that warm, summer evening, I was edified by the large number of people who took time out of their vacation to attend Mass. While a few were obviously local residents, it was apparent that most of the people in church were visitors from other parts of the country, even other nations. In the congregation were young couples (I imagined them to be on their honeymoon), families with restless kids and sullen teenagers, college students participating silently, senior citizens, and folks with disabilities for whom it was a real personal sacrifice to attend Mass. But there they were!

Reflecting on the assembly I asked myself, "Why do these people come to Mass Sunday after Sunday? What are they looking for? What do they want? What do they need?"

I believe, first of all, that people come to Mass on Sunday to be part of the Church, part of the Christian community. Please understand that by community here I don't mean a "Hello, my name is ____, what's yours?" experience, but something far more profound, an ecclesial community. Sometimes in the practice of liturgy we confuse the two.

The last time I attended Mass on vacation, the priest began by announcing: "As we begin today, folks, let's take a few minutes to get acquainted with the people around you. Tell your neighbor your name, where you're from, and what you do for a living." And so the congregation sat down for this banal banter while the priest assumed his talk-show host persona and worked the middle aisle greeting people. Please . . . that's not community; that's a cocktail party!

People want to belong to a Church community to be with and pray with other people who share their faith, their moral values, their liturgical practice. They want spiritual companions who will break bread with them and accompany them on their life's journey. Ecclesial community doesn't depend on personal, intimate knowledge of others, but on shared vision and faith. As a member of the Church, I am in community with people I'll never know, never meet. We are brothers and sisters in Christ, nonetheless.

Second, it seems to me that people come to Mass on Sunday because they long to hear the Word of God preached with conviction and enthusiasm. They want homilies that are doctrinally sound, personally prepared, and relevant to contemporary life.

I frequently hear the complaint that Catholic preaching has lost its spark, its zeal, that it has become too bland, cerebral, and generic. Good preaching, on the other hand, needs to be clear, direct, and simple. People seek moral guidance and want to learn the tenets of our faith. They want to hear about the Ten Commandments, justice and peace, human life and family relationships, final judgment, and eternal salvation.

In short, the faithful want preachers to preach as Jesus did, with power and conviction, challenging people, not avoiding difficult issues. People should leave Sunday Mass motivated to live the Gospel throughout the week, but confident they possess the spiritual means to do so.

Third, Catholics come to Mass on Sunday because they want to receive the Eucharist. This is a foundational element of Catholic life. Although national surveys have suggested that many Catholics lack proper understanding about the manner of Christ's presence in the Eucharist, I'm convinced that most practicing Catholics have a core belief that the Eucharist is really the Body of Christ. This "Holy Communion" is extremely important for them. Most members of the Church, while being unable perhaps to articulate the exact theology, know that the Mass is related to the Last Supper of Holy Thursday as well as the Cross of Good Friday.

It's true that our celebration and reception of the Eucharist is far too casual at times. It's true that we've tended to neglect the wonderful presence of Christ in the tabernacles of our churches. But I don't think our carelessness is a crisis of faith as much as a manifestation of our normal human nature. After all, we take many of our best gifts for granted all the time. Catholics believe in the Eucharist and fully realize its importance for their spiritual lives. That's one of the reasons they keep coming to Mass.

Finally, I believe Catholics come to Mass to find sanctuary from the turmoil of daily existence. Our lives are active, busy, and noisy—but empty. We come to Mass to be refreshed, to find peace, quiet, and fulfillment. Catholics come to church on Sundays to pray, not party, to converse with God, not chitchat with their neighbors.

The church is, or should be, a true sanctuary. I'm convinced that some semblance of sacred silence is crucial, even when the community gathers together. I'm troubled that some of our churches have a free-for-all before Mass, with loud and distracting conversations and laughter, making it nearly impossible for people to pray, to be recollected before they enter into the presence of the holy.

The recently revised *General Instruction of the Roman Missal* makes the same point:

> Even before the celebration itself, it is praiseworthy for silence to be observed in church, in the sacristy, and in adjacent areas, so that all may dispose themselves for the sacred rites which are to be enacted in a devout and fitting manner (no. 45).

People have enough, indeed, far too much noise in their lives, and the pilgrimage to church on Sundays should be peaceful, restful, and refreshing. Churches should be spiritual oases in the midst of our secular desert.

So, authentic community, effective preaching, the Eucharist, and sanctuary—these are the things Catholics are seeking when they come to Mass on Sunday. It's what they need for a faithful living-out of their Christian vocation. It's what the Church should give them.

On Holy Ground

In 1997 I visited a local Hindu temple to participate in the annual Interfaith Unity Day observance. Upon entering the building, all the participants were asked to remove their shoes. We remained shoeless throughout the day. Our Hindu guests explained to us their belief that the temple is sacred space and the removal of shoes is to prevent any contamination from the outside world from entering the realm of the sacred.

Although walking around in public without shoes was culturally uncomfortable for me, I came away from that experience with profound admiration for the Hindus' sense of the sacred. The exercise also prompted me to reflect again on our own Catholic practices, and to ask if we are losing a sense of the sacred in many of our practices and habits. I believe we are.

Our casual attitude about the sacred is reflected in so many ways. We certainly don't observe Sundays and holy days the way we used to. And how often do we hear people taking God's name in vain? And how commonly do we see the crucifix used only as jewelry rather than a religious symbol?

Our understanding of churches also reveals our sense of the sacred. As Catholics we use churches for two purposes. The one that tends to be emphasized today is to see the church as the building where God's people assemble. This we could call the horizontal dimension of our churches. Here we come together to share our faith stories, to support one another, and to form a Christian community that reaches out to the world. This is certainly a valid concept.

But another aspect of our church buildings should elicit the vertical dimension of our religious experience. In other words, we do not simply come together to be with other people—we already do that all the time. Rather, we come to church specifically because we believe that God is there, and in a particular way in the Most Blessed Sacrament. This is one of the primary beliefs of our Catholic faith: the Real Presence of Christ in the Blessed Sacrament. Respect for the divine Presence has characterized the Catholic Church for centuries and ought still to be an important part of our Catholic practice.

Entering Catholic churches used to be an impressive encounter with the transcendent. The senses were filled with the presence of God: the awesome silence, the soaring arches, the flickering candles, the aroma of incense, the beautiful stained-glass windows, the impressive statues. All were reminders that we had entered sacred space. Catholics didn't remove their shoes upon entering the church, but we did genuflect, not too proud in those days to bend our knee in adoration of the Supreme Being.

Even when it was full of people, the church was silent. The silence was a recognition of the presence of Jesus in the Blessed Sacrament. It provided a respite, a spiritual oasis in the midst of a very noisy, secular world. Our silence also allowed other people to reflect and pray so that they too might be in communion with God.

How about the way we dress these days for church? This is an especially timely point during the summer months when our clothing becomes more casual. Call me old fashioned if you wish, but I still think there's a difference between going to a picnic or a ball game and going to Mass on Sunday! Is it too much to ask that we dress respectfully and modestly when we go to church? Our attire is an expression of our reverence for God and the holy mysteries we celebrate. Some people say, "God doesn't care how we dress." I disagree. God does care how we dress, how we present ourselves before Him. God has made it rather clear that He expects us to respect His person, His name, and His house!

Our attire is also a mark of respect for our fellow worshipers. Some people are distracted by our cutoff shorts and tank tops. Some grow faint at the sight of our flabby, hairy bodies kneeling in front of them. Proper dress is often an expression of charity as much as modesty, a sign of respect for both God and our brothers and sisters.

How do we treat the church property itself? Do we care for it as the House of God it truly is? To visit a church after Sunday Masses is sometimes not a lot different from visiting a public park after a Fourth of July picnic. It's not at all unusual to find plastic bags filled with Cheerios, candy wrappers, used Kleenex, and soiled disposable diapers, the remnants of people on the run, people who couldn't wait to get out and get home.

And nothing speaks more eloquently about our reverence for the sacred than the manner in which we handle the Blessed Sacrament. Remember what Catholics believe about the Eucharist: That through the power of the priest and the action of the Holy Spirit, the bread and wine become truly the Body and Blood of our Lord Jesus Christ, Son of God, Second Person of the Holy Trinity. We believe that each drop of consecrated wine is the very Blood of Christ, that each fragment of consecrated bread is the Body of Christ.

In light of our belief in the reality of the Eucharist, then, several questions arise.

First, when we approach the altar of the Lord in Holy Communion, do we receive Jesus carefully, prayerfully, attentively? Do we spend some time with the Lord in personal prayer after Holy Communion?

And how do those of us who serve as ministers of the Eucharist—both ordinary and extraordinary—handle and distribute the sacred mysteries entrusted to us? Are we always careful and reverent, or do we sometimes become a little too casual? Are we respectful when we consume the excess Eucharist; and when we purify the sacred vessels, does it become simply a matter of "doing the dishes"? Are we mindful of the Eucharistic particles, the "crumbs," that remain after the breaking of the bread and distribution of Holy Communion, knowing that these fragments, too, even the tiniest of them, are still the Body of Christ?

In the Eucharist, God has given us the most sacred of all possible gifts, the gift of His own divine being. Therefore, we approach the Eucharist with the greatest of care, reverence, and love.

Many other examples could be cited, I'm sure, but the question remains: Are we as Catholics losing sight of the sacred, the transcendent in our lives? While it's true that reverence is primarily an interior attitude, it's also true that reverence is expressed and reinforced by external behaviors.

When God appeared to Moses in the burning bush, He instructed Moses, "Come no nearer! Remove the sandals from your feet, for the place where you stand is holy ground" (Ex. 3:5). While we do not live in Old Testament times, and while our tradition does not require us to remove our shoes, the fundamental reality is unchanged: We are commanded to have profound reverence for the sacred presence of God.

The Royal Road of the Holy Cross

One of my favorite sources of spiritual reading, especially during Lent and times of retreat, is *The Imitation of Christ*, the spiritual classic usually attributed to Thomas à Kempis in the fifteenth century. Some people believe that *The Imitation of Christ* is no longer relevant. They suggest that the theology and language is antiquated, narrow, and incomplete. I agree that the *Imitation* is not for everyone.

Nevertheless, the more I live and witness the troubles of our world, the more I am convinced that the *Imitation* contains great insight and enduring values. The concepts embodied in the *Imitation*, such as humility, obedience, sacrifice, prayer, and devotion to the Eucharist, are a perfect antidote to the evils of our age—the practical atheism, the materialism, the consumerism, the lack of fidelity to commitments, and the exaggerated emphasis on self.

One of the most compelling chapters of the *Imitation* is called "The Royal Road of the Holy Cross." It provides powerful reading for the season of Lent. Thomas à Kempis speaks about the futility of trying to avoid the Cross in our lives:

> Why then art thou afraid to take up thy cross, which leads to a kingdom? In the cross is salvation; in the cross is life; in the cross is protection from thy enemies. In the cross is infusion of heavenly sweetness; in the cross is strength of mind; in the cross is joy of spirit. In the cross is the height of virtue; in the

cross is the perfection of sanctity. There is no health of soul nor hope of eternal life but in the cross.[1]

Indeed there is no avoidance of the Cross, neither in faith nor in life. When Peter tempted Jesus to turn away from Jerusalem and thus avoid the Cross, Jesus sharply rebuked him. "Get behind me, Satan!" he said, "you are not on the side of God, but of men" (Mk. 8:33). Jesus Himself knew that there was no other road to glory but by the way of the Cross.

In our daily lives too, we learn that it is impossible to avoid the Cross. Everyone suffers, at one time or another, in one way or another. Anyone who has known the death of a child, a broken marriage vow, a debilitating and painful disease, the imprisonment of a loved one, or the struggle to support a family in difficult economic times, knows the reality of the Cross.

> Dispose and order all things according as thou wilt and as seems best to thee, and thou wilt still find something to suffer, either willingly or unwillingly, and so thou shalt still find the cross. . . . The cross, therefore, is always ready and everywhere waits for thee. Thou canst not escape it, whithersoever thou runnest; for whithersoever thou goest thou carriest thyself with thee and shalt always find the cross. And everywhere thou must of necessity have patience, if thou desirest inward peace and wouldst merit an eternal crown.[2]

When confronted with pain and sorrow, a person has two alternatives: either to abandon God, turn away from others and become bitter and isolated, or to embrace the Cross of Jesus and see that moment as an opportunity for personal growth, for acts of faith and love.

---

[1] Thomas à Kempis, *The Imitation of Christ* (Milwaukee: Bruce Publishing Co., 1940), chap. 12.
[2] Ibid.

The Cross is not only an unavoidable part of life, it is also an essential part of our Catholic faith and devotion. The Holy Sacrifice of the Mass, the center of our Catholic lives, is just that—the Sacrifice of Jesus on the Cross. The altar is not just the table of the Last Supper, it is also the Cross of Good Friday, on which the Lamb of God was sacrificed.

The Stations of the Cross are a beautiful and meaningful part of our spiritual journey as Christians. Anyone who participates in the Stations of the Cross understands a little more clearly the extent of the suffering and death of Jesus and is therefore better prepared to celebrate the joy and peace of Easter Sunday.

Our little acts of penance and mortification during Lent help us to share in the Cross of Christ. They are little things to be sure, but any love relationship needs to be nourished by small acts and gentle deeds every day.

The Cross of Jesus is central to our churches. I personally have a preference for seeing crucifixes in our churches that depict the reality of the suffering Christ. Not just an empty cross, and not a cross with the glorified Christ, but a crucifix that depicts the suffering and sacrifice of Jesus. The sight of the crucified Christ always evokes, at least in me, a sense of immense gratitude and humility for all that Jesus has done.

As we prepare to enter into the mysteries of Holy Week and celebrate the great events of our redemption, let us prayerfully reflect on the Cross of Christ. Let us be bold enough to walk the royal road of the holy Cross:

> If, indeed, there had been anything better and more beneficial to man's salvation than suffering, Christ certainly would have showed it by word and example. For He manfully exhorts both His disciples that followed Him and all that desire to follow Him to bear the cross. . . . so that when we have read

and searched all let this be the final conclusion, that "through many tribulations we must enter into the kingdom of God" (Acts 14:21).[3]

---

[3] Ibid.

Receiving Holy Communion

At their 1996 fall meeting, the bishops of the United States approved revised guidelines for the reception of Holy Communion. This is the statement that is usually found on the inside cover of missalettes used in Catholic churches. The wording has now been revised to reflect recent liturgical and ecumenical statements, but the fundamental teaching of the Church on this matter has not changed. The basic principle is this: Only Catholics may receive Holy Communion, and Catholics who do receive Holy Communion must be properly disposed. Let's try to understand the consequences of this very important and sensitive issue.

The guidelines state, first of all, that "we welcome our fellow Christians to the celebration of the Eucharist as our brothers and sisters." The statement urges us to pray that the action of the Holy Spirit will overcome the sad divisions that have separated us. This is a clear realization that while Christians share a common faith, there are still significant issues and practices that keep us apart. Someday, God willing, they will be resolved.

The guidelines teach us, however, that

> because Catholics believe that the celebration of the Eucharist is a sign of the reality of the oneness of faith, life, and worship, members of those churches with whom we are not yet fully united are ordinarily not admitted to Holy Communion.

The guidelines point out that other Christians may receive Holy Communion in "exceptional" cases only with the specific permission of the bishop and only when very particular conditions are in place. From a Catholic perspective, members of Orthodox Churches and the Polish National Church may be permitted to receive Holy Communion. Sometimes, however, their own disciplines do not permit them to do so.

To some people, I am sure, these restrictions seem harsh and unnecessary, a violation of the ecumenical spirit of our age. The question is, "Why are there so many restrictions about receiving Holy Communion if people are of good will and the Eucharist is so helpful to us?" That's certainly a legitimate question, motivated by good intentions.

We should emphasize at the outset that the directive that only Catholics may receive Holy Communion is not a suggestion that Catholics are better or holier than other people. The reasons are more subtle than that.

The first reason, as the guidelines suggest, is that the reception of Holy Communion is not just an expression of belief in the Lord Jesus Christ, but also an indication of membership, "communion," in a particular Church, a Church that shares "oneness of faith, life, and worship." Unity among Christians is not yet complete, and the reception of Holy Communion in churches of other denominations ignores that important reality.

The second reason is that the reception of Holy Communion in a Catholic church presumes Catholic belief about the Eucharist. Catholics believe in the doctrine of transubstantiation, that the bread and wine become, in a substantial way, the Body and Blood of Christ. Catholics also believe that the Eucharist is a veritable sharing in the sacrifice of Christ on Calvary. Many of our fellow Christians, while having a high regard for the celebration of the Lord's Supper, do not share our belief in the substantial and sacrificial nature of the Eucharist. The reception of the Eucharist in a Catholic church presumes an acceptance of Catholic teaching as to what—or who—the Eucharist is.

Now perhaps you have heard that on special occasions, such as weddings and funerals, some priests will invite all those in the church, including those who are not Catholic, to receive Holy Communion. For reasons already cited, and for other good reasons, this practice is improper and theologically unsound. While a priest certainly might have good intentions—such as a desire to extend Christian hospitality, an ecumenical instinct, or the desire to avoid hard feelings—the invitation to everybody is inappropriate. Inviting members of other churches to receive Holy Communion shows a lack of respect for their beliefs and the beliefs of Catholics as well.

While the motivations for inviting everyone to Holy Communion might seem to be "ecumenical," in the long run the practice does more harm than good to authentic ecumenical relationships. The most detrimental thing we can possibly do to achieve legitimate Christian unity it to "paper over" our differences with other religions. It's somewhat akin to two people entering marriage before they've gotten to know each other, before they've resolved all their differences. A good marriage, in personal life or ecumenism, demands that differences have been courageously addressed and resolved, and that there be true understanding and acceptance by each party. That's the solid foundation on which the union can be built. Experience has taught that couples who live together without the benefit of marriage have a higher divorce rate than those who are more patient with their plans. An important lesson for our ecumenical endeavors, I believe!

I am convinced that a premature invitation to Holy Communion removes one of the most compelling incentives for people to join the Catholic Church. There are many stories, many true stories, of people being attracted to the Catholic

Church by our belief in the Eucharist, and their desire to receive the Eucharist. The Eucharist is the spiritual magnet that draws people to experience the riches of our Catholic faith. If anyone can receive the Eucharist, why bother joining the Church?

Another very serious pastoral problem that arises when priests invite non-Catholics to receive Holy Communion is the awkward situation it causes for those priests who try to follow the law of the Church. How many priests have been challenged by parishioners or visitors who say something like, "Father so-and-so is a really nice guy and he allows everyone to receive Holy Communion. Why don't you, Father?" This kind of liturgical inconsistency causes confusion for the faithful, scandal within the Church, and a real morale problem among the priests. In short, it's just not fair! (The same can be said, by the way, of other liturgical abuses.)

Only Catholics should receive Holy Communion, but we long for the day, and pray for the day, when authentic Christian unity will allow all Christians to meet at the Lord's table with clear understanding and good faith.

The guidelines also remind Catholics that the reception of Holy Communion is a great and holy privilege and that they too must be properly disposed. As the guidelines say:

> We are encouraged to receive Communion devoutly and frequently. In order to be properly disposed to receive Communion, participants should not be conscious of grave sin and normally should have fasted for one hour. . . . A frequent reception of the Sacrament of Penance is encouraged for all.

The point here is that in Holy Communion, we are receiving a precious gift, and while we know that we are never worthy to receive the Lord, we must be as well disposed as possible for this sacred encounter. Most people are very reverent in receiving Communion, and that is very edifying. But I, like perhaps many distributors of the Eucharist, am occasionally disturbed by the casual manner in which some people approach the altar of the Lord—half asleep, failing to respond, abruptly grabbing the sacred Host from the priest, talking to the person next to them, chewing gum. We need to examine our conscience in this matter: How do I receive the Body of Christ? And how do I distribute the Body of Christ?

Finally, in completing our survey of the guidelines, we note that they contain brief paragraphs addressed to non-Christians and to others who are not receiving Communion. These people are warmly welcomed to the liturgy and encouraged to "express in their hearts a prayerful desire for unity with the Lord Jesus" and to pray "for the peace and unity of the human family."

As early as New Testament times, Saint Paul reminded Christians about proper reverence in receiving the Body of Christ:

> Whoever, therefore, eats the bread or drinks the cup of the Lord in an unworthy manner will be guilty of profaning the body and blood of the Lord. Let a man examine himself, and so eat of the bread and drink of the cup (1 Cor. 11:27-28).

In that same spirit, let us resolve to receive Holy Communion often and to receive it well.

Totus Tuus

After one of our vocations dinners, a priest thanked me for the invitation and encouraged me to continue working for vocations to the priesthood. "Only one thing is lacking, Bishop," Father said. "You need to place this vocations program under the patronage of our Blessed Mother. Then you will know great success."

In a heartbeat, I knew he was exactly right. Our work of promoting vocations to the priesthood, as well as every work of the Church and of our lives, should be under the patronage of our Blessed Mother. The month of May is traditionally a time to rediscover that truth and to renew our special devotion to Mary.

Mary is the Mother of God. It is from that title that all the privileges enjoyed by Mary flow, privileges that comprise the body of Catholic teaching about Mary. Mary was chosen from the very beginning to play that essential role in salvation history, to be the Mother of God. For that reason, she was sinless from the moment of her conception and throughout her life. For that reason, she remained a virgin, before, during, and after the birth of Christ. For that reason, her body was assumed into the glory of heaven at the end of her earthly pilgrimage. Once we believe that God intervened in Mary's life in a miraculous and wonderful way, it shouldn't be difficult to believe all the other teachings of the Church about Mary.

Along with this Catholic doctrine about our Blessed Mother, there is also another very personal side of our devotion to Mary. It is this devotion, at least in part, that gives the Catholic faith such warmth and beauty.

Our Holy Father chose as his papal motto the words *Totus Tuus*, and in so doing committed his whole life and ministry to the care of our Blessed Mother. *Totus Tuus*—"I am completely yours, O Mary." The Holy Father has found great inspiration and protection under the patronage of our Blessed Mother, especially in the times of suffering that have marked his pontificate.

But isn't that true of many Catholics? Haven't we, for generations, found comfort and guidance in our prayers to our Blessed Mother? Mary completely understands the human condition, because she was completely human, subject to all the trials and tribulations of our earthly journey. Mary surely knew the same successes and failures, joys and sorrows, pleasures and pains that are part of our lives, and perhaps even more so.

Mary herself was a widowed mother. Mary knew what it meant to have a son rejected by society, imprisoned and condemned. Mary knew poverty and exile, and was herself marginalized by the culture of her time.

But how did she respond? With a plaintive cry about how unfair life was, a wailing about her rights, privileges, and personal needs? Not at all. Mary responded to the challenges of life with heroic courage, faith, and trust, confident of her place in the world and God's place in her life. "[H]e who is mighty has done great things for me, and holy is his name" (Lk. 1:48).

Mary's virtues serve as a beautiful and timely example for Christians of our age. To a society consumed by sexual excess, Mary speaks of purity and virginity. To an age of commercialism and materialism, Mary speaks of faith and trust. In a world filled with the wreckage of broken marriages and families, Mary points us to the Holy Family, bonded together in mutual respect and love centered on the Lord Jesus.

Catholics in every generation have turned to Mary in prayer, in liturgy, in devotions, especially the Rosary, and have found in that harbor an unshakable model of strength, gentleness, courage, and trust.

When I was a little boy growing up in the Laurel Gardens section of Pittsburgh, I had a May altar in my room, a beautiful little grotto of the Blessed Mother adorned each year with the finest dandelions I could find. Humble, but sincere.

So it is with our lives. We come to Mary full of devotion and love, with the best of intentions, but all that we can really offer are the humble flowers of our own very imperfect spiritual gardens.

My guess is that Mary is pleased nonetheless. Mothers are always pleased by the simple pictures drawn by their children, so much so that they are proudly displayed on the refrigerator doors of America. Not great works of art—just great works of love. Mothers instinctively know that it is the effort that counts. So I am sure that Mary is very pleased with our prayer, devotion, and virtue, as simple and imperfect as they might be!

I ask Mary our Mother to bless our work of promoting vocations to the priesthood and religious life, and I ask her to bless all the works of our hands.

Let us join our Holy Father in praying to Mary, our Blessed Mother.

Totus Tuus. I am completely yours, O Mary!

The Rosary: The Mysteries of Life

October 7 is the Feast of Our Lady of the Rosary, highlighting the month dedicated in a special way to the wonderful prayer that is such a beautiful part of Catholic faith and devotion.

Although the roots of this prayer form are ancient, even pre-Christian, the Rosary as we know it today dates back to Saint Dominic (1170-1221). Later, on October 7, 1571, Pope Pius V declared that because of the spiritual assistance of the Rosary in securing victory over the Turks at Lepanto, a commemoration in honor of the Rosary would be held each year on that date. The Rosary has maintained a special place in the Church ever since and has been promoted by popes throughout the centuries, including our present Holy Father, John Paul II.

As we enter a new millennium and new chapter in the history of the Church, the Rosary remains firmly grounded in the popular devotion of Catholics, accompanying them in moments of joy and sorrow, life and death. It is a source of powerful intercession for Catholic faithful who seek Mary's consolation and assistance in every imaginable personal and spiritual need.

The Rosary is, without a doubt, an effective means of spiritual growth, a prayer of contemplation, setting before us the faithful example of Mary our Mother, leading us closer to Jesus our Savior. When we pray the Rosary we reflect upon the mysteries, the principal events, of the lives of Mary and Jesus. As such, it is a short course in salvation history, a Bible in miniature.

I've often thought that the Rosary helps us to reflect upon and find meaning in the joyful, sorrowful, and glorious moments of our own lives, placing all we do in a spiritual context.

Joyful Mysteries

The Annunciation—As we consider the announcement that Mary had been chosen to be the Mother of God, we are reminded that we, too, are called to participate in God's plan of salvation, each of us in some particular, unique way. We do so by a faithful living out of the vocation God has given us.

The Visitation—Mary hastened to Elizabeth to share the good news of God's initiative in her life and to be with Elizabeth during her own time of need. Simple acts of kindness, thoughtfulness—we need to extend them to others, particularly to our friends and families, those with whom we live and work every day, those whom we most often take for granted.

The Nativity—"And the Word became flesh and dwelt among us" (Jn. 1:14). The birth of Jesus reminds us of God's love for the human race. The birth of Jesus teaches us how special human life is. The birth of each child is a sign that God hasn't yet given up on the human race!

The Presentation—Simeon and Anna were faithful people whose faith and love for God were deep and constant, enabling them to recognize the child Jesus as the "light for revelation to the Gentiles, and for glory to thy people Israel" (Lk. 2:32). How many times and in how many ways have we been blessed by the unexpected appearance of God in our lives?

The Finding in the Temple—How Joseph and Mary worried when they could not find Jesus among their relatives as they returned home from Jerusalem. How they rejoiced when they found Him in the Temple. Have you been separated from family and friends by geography or personal animosity?

How much joy there is when we are reconciled to loved ones from whom we have been separated!

Sorrowful Mysteries

The Agony in the Garden—The agony of Jesus was caused by the knowledge that His "hour had come," that He was about to endure intense pain and suffering for the love of God and mankind. Thus He prayed, "Father, if thou art willing, remove this cup from me" (Lk. 22:42). At times we've agonized over the uncertainty of life, over difficult, painful, even life-changing decisions. In those moments, have we been supported by our friends? In those moments, did God send an angel to minister to us?

The Scourging at the Pillar—Pontius Pilate thought that the scourging of Jesus would be enough to satisfy the crowd, but "they were urgent, demanding with loud cries that he should be crucified" (Lk. 23:23). Have there been times at work or school, at home or in relationships, when you've given your best, done all you can, only to have others say it wasn't enough? The Scourging at the Pillar teaches us of the need for patience, perseverance, and strength in all the circumstances of our lives.

The Crowning of Thorns—As the soldiers wove a crown of sharp thorns and forced it onto the head of Jesus, they also taunted Him, ridiculing Him and His mission. If you are a faithful Christian, surely there have been times when the practice of your faith has been questioned, doubted, and ridiculed. Welcome the opportunities you encounter to witness to your faith in Jesus Christ!

The Carrying of the Cross—As Jesus labored to carry His Cross through the streets of Jerusalem, the reaction of the crowd was mixed. Some ignored Him, going about their daily affairs; some blasphemed Him; but some, like Simon of Cyrene and Veronica, came to His assistance. What has been your greatest suffering? Have good people come forward to minister to you during those difficult times?

The Crucifixion—The Crucifixion of Jesus reminds us of the sheer agony of intense, unrelenting physical pain. Perhaps you've experienced the torture of physical pain caused by an accident or illness, a pain that turns every movement, every moment into a true cross. In imitation of our Lord Jesus, are you able to make such moments expressions of faith?

Glorious Mysteries

The Resurrection—The Resurrection of Christ is proof that when all is said and done, light is stronger than darkness, life stronger than death. The Resurrection makes our lives a constant springtime. Thanks be to God that we know so many moments of resurrection, moments of joy and victory, success and satisfaction, light and life.

The Ascension—"Christ, the mediator between God and man, judge of the world and Lord of all, has passed beyond our sight, not to abandon us, but to be our hope" (*Sacramentary*). When you think of your personal future, what emotion do you experience—uncertainty, anxiety, fear? The Ascension of Jesus reminds us that we should always anticipate the future with hope and unbounded confidence.

The Descent of the Holy Spirit—At the Last Supper Jesus promised His disciples: "I will pray the Father, and he will give you another Counselor, to be with you for ever, even the Spirit of truth, whom the world cannot receive. . . . I will not leave you desolate; I will come to you" (Jn. 14:16, 18). That promise was fulfilled on Pentecost Day. Recall that the Holy Spirit is God's constant presence with you. Nothing "will be able to separate us from the love of God in Christ Jesus our Lord" (Rom. 8:39).

The Assumption of Mary—At the end of her earthly life, Mary was assumed body and soul into heaven. The

Assumption is yet another reminder that there is indeed life after death. Think of and pray for your loved ones, your family and friends who have passed away. Pray with gratitude for their lives on earth and with confidence that they may share in the glory of heaven in perfect peace and joy.

The Coronation of Mary as Queen of Heaven—"[A]t your right hand stands the queen in gold" (Ps. 45:9). Mary is our Mother and powerful friend who stands at the right hand of God. We should never hesitate, for even a moment, to turn to Mary and seek her assistance.

> Remember, O most gracious Virgin Mary, that never was it known that anyone who fled to your protection, implored your help, or sought your intercession was left unaided. . . . In your mercy, hear and answer us. Amen.

V

In Union
with the Pope

John Paul the Great

"And I tell you, you are Peter, and on this rock I will build my church" (Mt. 16:18).

With those few words, following upon Saint Peter's profession of faith, Jesus gave human form and definitive structure to the Church and placed Saint Peter as her head. Saint Peter eventually moved to Rome, taking his primacy with him, and from that time on, the Bishop of Rome has been the visible head of the Church on earth.

Through the centuries the papacy has been filled with thoroughly human leaders. Most popes have been holy men, men in love with Christ and His people, men of great learning and holiness. Other popes have not lived up to the dignity of their office. I have no hesitation, however, in saying that Pope John Paul II is one of the great popes in the history of the Church and one of the most significant leaders of the past century.

Even secular sources confirm the greatness, the historical dimensions of this man. A 1996 biography, *His Holiness*, written by Carl Bernstein and Marco Politi, makes the point:

> When John Paul II took control of the Church, its influence and power in the world were widely believed to be declining. But Wojtyla saw himself as a man called upon by destiny, by God, to change the face of the Church and the world. . . . As Pope, he became one of the most remarkable figures of the second half of the 20th century.

When *TIME* magazine chose John Paul II as its Person of the Year some time ago, the author of the *TIME* profile wrote:

People who see him—and countless of millions have—do not forget him. His appearances generate an electricity unmatched by anyone else on earth. When he talks, it is not only to his flock of nearly a billion; he expects the world to listen.

John Paul's impact on the world has already been enormous, ranging from the global to the personal. His power rests on the word, not the sword. As he has demonstrated throughout the 16 years of his papacy, John Paul needs no divisions. He is an army of one.

The great Protestant preacher, the Reverend Billy Graham, says that the pope will "go down in history as the greatest of the modern popes. He's been the strong voice of conscience of the whole Christian world."

The testimonies about this pope could go on and on, but there is no doubt that John Paul II has changed the history of the world and the Church as few others before him have done.

As Catholics, however, we see the pope not simply as a great world leader, but as an integral part of our faith. John Paul II is the successor of Saint Peter, the Supreme Pastor, the Vicar of Christ, our Holy Father. In the context of our Catholic family, the celebration of the pope's golden jubilee a few years ago was a significant event not only for him, but for all of us.

John Paul II is a pilgrim and a pastor to the world, a good shepherd who travels throughout the world bringing the Gospel of Christ and the spiritual blessings of the Church to Catholics, other Christians, people of other faiths, and non-believers. His wonderful celebrations of World Youth Day have touched millions of young people who find in him a beacon of truth and integrity.

John Paul II is a prophet whose voice, more than any other of our time, has spoken constantly and passionately about human rights, human dignity, and justice. Like most prophets, he has suffered for his courage.

John Paul II is an effective diplomat, taking his place on the political stage of the world, standing for peace and freedom, contributing to the demise of Communism in eastern Europe, not through violent revolution, but through peaceful evolution.

John Paul II is a brilliant teacher, whose words will be read a thousand years from now alongside the words of Augustine, Aquinas, and Teresa of Avila. His encyclicals and apostolic letters will have a profound and lasting impact on the Church and the world: *Evangelium Vitae*, on the sanctity of human life; *Veritatis Splendor*, on the importance of objective moral truth; *Ut Unum Sint*, in which he voices an urgent call for Christian unity; *Vita Consecrata*, in which he points the way to a renewal of religious life in the Church; and *Novo Millennio Ineunte*, in which he provides a comprehensive and beautiful pastoral plan for the Church in the new millennium.

John Paul II is a source of unity within the Church and with the Church, insisting rightly on discipline for members of the Church and calling insistently for unity with other Christians, especially Orthodox Christians, as a necessary manifestation of the will of Christ.

Quite a curriculum vitae which the pope has assembled. But what does the pope himself say about his ministry in his book *Crossing the Threshold of Hope?*

> Against this background (the death and resurrection of Christ), expressions such as "Supreme Pontiff," "Your Holiness," and "Holy Father" are of little importance. What is important originates in the death and resurrection of Jesus. What is important is that which comes from the power of the Holy Spirit.
>
> From this perspective, the expression "Vicar of Christ" assumes its true meaning. More than dignity, it alludes to service. It emphasizes the duties of the Pope in the Church, his Petrine ministry, carried out for the good of the Church and the faithful.

From these personal reflections we see that the pope claims little credit for himself, but holds in great esteem the office which he fulfills. It is that understanding of the responsibility and impact of his office that has led our Holy Father to a total act of self-giving in his life and ministry.

There are some who disregard our Holy Father and disdain his teaching. One can only speculate why they are so threatened by this good and humble man. There are some who hope that after his death, the teachings of the Church will be changed—teachings such as the prohibition of contraception, the permanence of marriage, the condemnation of abortion, the affirmation of a male-only ministerial priesthood. How foolish these hopes! John Paul didn't create these truths; he didn't simply bring them with him from Poland. But what he has done is to maintain and explain the teachings of the Church handed down over the centuries from one generation to the next. Those who believe that these teachings will change with the death of John Paul completely misunderstand the history of the Church and the role of papacy. They will be bitterly disappointed!

I love Pope John Paul II and will always revere his ministry in the Church. My own life has been changed by this pope in ways I could never have imagined. This is the pope who called to me to be a bishop and sent me to serve the Church in Youngstown. For both of these special opportunities I shall be always grateful.

We reserve the title "the Great" for popes who have changed history, those who have made a lasting impact on the Church and the world: Gregory the Great, Leo the Great. Is there any doubt that someday the world will refer to this pope as "John Paul the Great"?

We often wish that we could have lived in the times of the apostles and other great saints. In the person of John Paul II, we are!

Having Great Sundays

"We might not be Dairy Queen, but our Sundays are great!" That's the very clever message I once saw on the bulletin board of a local Protestant church. Having great Sundays should be the goal of every Christian community. It's also the very important message of the 1998 apostolic letter, *Dies Domini* (The Day of the Lord), written by our Holy Father, Pope John Paul II.

Remember when most Catholics made a very serious effort to attend Mass on Sunday and knew it was a grave sin if they didn't? Remember when most stores and businesses closed on Sundays so that families could spend some time together? Remember when we worried about how long we could do "servile work" on Sundays before a venial sin became mortal? While some of these concerns seem quaint by today's moral standards, there is no doubt that we really have lost a sense of the sacred, particularly in regard to "keeping holy the Lord's Day."

To counter this trend, and to help the Church recapture the special meaning of Sunday, the pope has written this letter which, from the viewpoint of practical Christianity, is as important as any other he's written.

In the introduction of *Dies Domini*, the Holy Father lays the groundwork for the themes he will address throughout the letter. It is, of course, the Resurrection of Christ on the first day of the week that makes Sunday so special for Christians:

> Those who have received the grace of faith in the Risen Lord cannot fail to grasp the significance of this day of the week

with the same deep emotion which led Saint Jerome to say, "Sunday is the day of the Resurrection, it is the day of Christians, it is our day" (no. 2).

The introduction goes on to discuss how the observance of Sunday as a holy day has been replaced by the more secular observance of the "weekend":

> The custom of the "weekend" has become more widespread, a weekly period of respite, spent perhaps far from home and often involving participation in cultural, political or sporting activities. . . . Unfortunately, when Sunday loses its funda-mental meaning and becomes merely part of a "weekend," it can happen that people stay locked within a horizon so limited that they can no longer see "the heavens" (no. 4).

The first chapter of the letter is entitled *Dies Domini* and relates the observance of the Lord's Day to the Sabbath of the Chosen People of Israel. The creation narrative reminds us that God Himself rested on the seventh day, the Sabbath:

> The divine rest of the seventh day does not allude to an inactive God, but emphasizes the fullness of what has been accomplished. It speaks, as it were, of God's lingering before the "very good" work (Gen. 1:31) which his hand has wrought, in order to cast upon it *a gaze full of joyous delight* (no. 11, original emphasis).

The Sabbath, therefore, sanctified by God, becomes the Lord's Day par excellence. It is a day of remembering the mighty works of the Lord, the day on which men and women represent the voice of all creation, offering praise and thanksgiving to the Creator.

In the second chapter, *Dies Christi* (The Day of Christ), the letter explains the reasons for the transition of the holy day from the seventh day, the Sabbath, to the first day of the week, Sunday. "We celebrate Sunday because of the venerable Resurrection of our Lord Jesus Christ, and we do so not only at Easter but also at each turning of the week," wrote Pope Innocent I, at the beginning of the fifth century.

The letter points to the great sacrifices early Christians had to make to observe the Lord's Day. Because of their vibrant faith, they did so:

> In those early Christian times, the weekly rhythm of days was generally not part of life in the regions where the Gospel spread. . . . For Christians, therefore, it was very difficult to observe the Lord's Day on a set day each week. This explains why the faithful had to gather before sunrise (no. 22).

This second chapter concludes with a clear statement:

> Given its many meanings and aspects, and its links to the very foundations of the faith, the celebration of the Christian Sunday remains, on the threshold of the Third Millennium, an indispensable element of our Christian identity (no. 30).

The third chapter, *Dies Ecclesiae*, teaches that Sunday is also the Day of the Church. "Those who have received the grace of baptism are not saved as individuals alone, but as members of the Mystical Body, having become part of the People of God" (no. 31).

This incorporation into the Body of Christ is accomplished in its fullest way through the celebration of the Sunday Eucharist:

> The Eucharist feeds and forms the Church. . . . At Sunday Mass, Christians relive with particular intensity the experience of the Apostles on the evening of Easter when the Risen Lord appeared to them as they were gathered together (nos. 32-33).

In this context the pope reminds the Church of the serious obligation to participate in Mass on Sunday:

> Since the Eucharist is the very heart of Sunday, it is clear why, from the earliest centuries, the Pastors of the Church have not ceased to remind the faithful of *the need to take part in the liturgical assembly*. . . . [O]ne should never forget the genuine heroism of priests and faithful who have fulfilled this obligation even when faced with danger and the denial of religious freedom. . . . Because the faithful are obliged to attend Mass unless there is a grave impediment, Pastors have the corresponding duty to offer to everyone the real possibility of fulfilling the precept (nos. 46, 49, original emphasis).

Dies Hominis (The Day of Man), the fourth chapter, expands on some of the more human dimensions of the Lord's Day. It is a day of Christian joy, a day of special celebration for God's people. It is a day of rest:

> For Christians it is not normal that Sunday, the day of joyful celebration, should not also be a day of rest, and it is difficult for them to keep Sunday holy if they do not have enough free time (no. 64).

This rest is sacred time because it is a way of withdrawing from the difficult demands of daily life in order to renew our awareness that ultimately everything is a work of God.

This chapter also reminds us that Sunday is to be a day of Christian solidarity with the poor:

> The Sunday Eucharist, therefore, not only does not absolve the faithful from the duties of charity, but on the contrary commits them even more "to the works of charity, of mercy, of apostolic outreach . . ." (no. 69).

"[W]hy not make the Lord's day a more intense time of sharing . . . ? Inviting to a meal people who are alone, visiting the sick, providing food for needy families, spending a few hours in voluntary work and acts of solidarity" (no. 72) are all effective ways of bringing the love of Christ into people's lives.

The final chapter, *Dies Dierum* (The Day of Days), points to our future as Christians. Sunday is the day which reveals the meaning of time itself:

> The Christian Sunday is wholly other! Springing from the Resurrection, it cuts through human time, the months, the years, the centuries, like a directional arrow which points them towards their target: Christ's Second Coming (no. 75).

While it is difficult for mankind to have a complete picture of the future, Christians have a key role to play in that regard. "Keeping Sunday holy is the important witness which they are called to bear, so that every stage of human history will be upheld by hope" (no. 75).

The conclusion summarizes the dominant themes of the message and places Sunday observance within the context of the celebration of the Great Jubilee of the Year 2000:

> The spiritual and pastoral riches of Sunday, as it has been handed on to us by tradition, are truly great. When its significance and implications are understood in their entirety, Sunday in a way becomes a synthesis of the Christian life and a condition for living it well (no. 81).

And again,

> the imminence of the Jubilee invites us to a deeper spiritual and pastoral commitment. . . . As the weekly "solemnity," however, Sunday will continue to shape the time of the Church's pilgrimage, until that Sunday which will know no evening (no. 87).

This brief summary cannot begin to capture the richness and full impact of the pope's apostolic letter on the Lord's Day. It is my fervent hope and prayer, however, that we as Catholics will carefully consider its message so that we will always have "great Sundays," days that will be the cornerstone of our communal life and Christian faith.

Saint Joseph, Promise Keeper

The Solemnity of Saint Joseph on March 19 is a beautiful and important feast day in the Church. In preparing a few thoughts for this occasion, I was reminded that about a decade ago our Holy Father, Pope John Paul II, wrote an apostolic exhortation about Saint Joseph entitled *Redemptoris Custos* (Guardian of the Redeemer). It may be one of the least known of the pope's writings, but it serves as a fruitful source of reflection on this great saint.

In the introduction to his letter, the pope explains the purpose of his writing about Saint Joseph, "that all may grow in devotion to the Patron of the Universal Church and in love for the Savior whom he served in such an exemplary manner." The document goes on then to study the image of Saint Joseph from several different perspectives of Scripture and Tradition.

What portrait of Saint Joseph emerges from the Gospels? In studying the narratives of Saint Matthew and Saint Luke, it is obvious that the importance of Saint Joseph in salvation history is closely linked to that of the Virgin Mary. Joseph and Mary had not consummated their marriage when suddenly Mary was found to be with child. Joseph had to confront the reality of Mary's pregnancy without the full insight of Christian revelation we enjoy today. The pope writes that Joseph

> did not know how to deal with Mary's "astonishing" motherhood. He certainly sought an answer to this unsettling question, but above all he sought a way out of what was for him a difficult situation (no. 3).

It was at this moment, however, that the angel of the Lord appeared to Joseph in a dream and said:

> Joseph, son of David, do not fear to take Mary your wife, for that which is conceived in her is of the Holy Spirit; she will bear a son, and you shall call his name Jesus, for he will save his people from their sins (Mt. 1:20-21).

From that point Joseph realized that Mary's pregnancy was the result of extraordinary divine intervention, and he understood that he too was about to play a special role in God's plan for salvation. Joseph now had no hesitation about taking care of Mary and her unborn son. "In this way he showed a readiness of will like Mary's with regard to what God asked of him through the angel" (no. 3).

When Mary visited her cousin Elizabeth, she heard the words of Elizabeth addressed to her: "[B]lessed is she who believed that there would be a fulfillment of what was spoken to her from the Lord" (Lk. 1:45). In a certain sense, the pope writes, the blessedness ascribed to Mary "can be referred to Joseph as well, since he responded positively to the Word of God when it was communicated to him at the decisive moment." Now, at the beginning of this spiritual journey, "the faith of Mary meets the faith of Joseph" (no. 4).

The key to Joseph's participation in the divine mystery is found in his "service of fatherhood":

> It was to assure fatherly protection for Jesus that God chose Joseph to be Mary's spouse. . . . While clearly affirming that Jesus was conceived by the power of the Holy Spirit, and that virginity remained intact in the marriage, the evangelists refer to Joseph as Mary's husband and to Mary as his wife (no. 7).

Joseph's fatherhood, then, was not of the biological type, and Pope John Paul II quotes Pope Paul VI in explaining the exact nature of his fatherhood:

His fatherhood is expressed concretely "in his having made his life a service, a sacrifice to the mystery of the Incarnation, and to the redemptive mission connected with it; in having used the legal authority which was his over the Holy Family in order to make a total gift of self, of his life and work; in having turned his human vocation to domestic love into a superhuman oblation of self, an oblation of his heart and all his abilities into love placed at the service of the Messiah growing up in his house" (no. 8).

How completely Joseph fulfilled his responsibilities as a father is clearly seen in the Scriptures, from the birth of Jesus, His circumcision, the conferral of His name, the presentation in the Temple, the flight into Egypt, the finding in the Temple, and the support and education of Jesus at Nazareth.

Saint Joseph is frequently referred to as the "just man," a title that reveals that he "bore within himself the entire heritage of the Old Covenant" (no. 32). Joseph made a conscious decision not to interfere in the plan of God which was coming to pass, and he obeyed the explicit command of the angel, allowing God's plan to come to fulfillment. It is this special sacrifice of Joseph and his total trust in God that allows him to be characterized as the "just man."

It is interesting to note that the Gospels do not record even a single spoken word of Joseph, but his silence has its own special eloquence, for it permits us to see Joseph's role in relationship to Mary and to God.

The same aura of silence that envelops everything else about Joseph also shrouds his work as a carpenter in the house of Nazareth. It is, however, a silence that reveals in a special way the inner portrait of the man. . . . [I]n Joseph, the apparent tension between the active and the contemplative life finds an ideal harmony that is only possible for those who possess the perfection of charity (nos. 25, 27).

Saint Joseph the carpenter is venerated as the patron of work, and in his common life, Joseph points to the "sanctification of daily life, a sanctification which each person must acquire according to his or her own state" (no. 24). As Paul VI wrote, "St. Joseph is the model of those humble ones that Christianity raises up to great destinies."

Finally, the Holy Father invokes Saint Joseph as the patron saint of the Universal Church. He explains that as Saint Joseph protected the Holy Family of Nazareth, to this day he protects the holy family that is the Church of God.

> This patronage must be invoked as ever necessary for the Church, not only as a defense against all dangers, but also, and indeed primarily, as an impetus for her renewed commitment to evangelization in the world (no. 29).

Thus the Church turns to Saint Joseph and his "noble example which transcends all individual states of life and serves as a model for the entire Christian community" (no. 30).

Having reviewed this portrait of Saint Joseph in *Redemptoris Custos*, we can ask, "What are the practical lessons we learn from the life and service of Saint Joseph?" Well, we are reminded, first of all, of the importance of doing God's will in our lives, even when it is difficult and demanding. Joseph points to the lasting value of family life with Christ as its center, the place where each person grows in age, grace, and wisdom. Joseph teaches the meaning of purity and chastity that are so absent from the common life of society today. From Saint Joseph we learn the value of our daily work, that *what* we do isn't as important as *how* we do it. And Saint Joseph reminds us of the sanctity of the Church, the Body of Christ, and how good it is for believers to have special love and reverence for the Church.

In recent years we've heard a great deal about an organization called Promise Keepers, a group of men who have renewed their commitments to God and their families. In light of all we know about Saint Joseph, I think it's fair to name him the first and finest "promise keeper." He was faithful to God and he totally fulfilled all the commitments that were his. As we celebrate his feast day, may we follow his example and be blessed by his intercession. Saint Joseph, pray for us!

The Genius of Women

Women's dignity has often been unacknowledged and their prerogatives misrepresented; they have often been relegated to the margins of society and even reduced to servitude. This has prevented women from truly being themselves and it has resulted in a spiritual impoverishment of humanity.

These are the very challenging words of one of the world's most radical feminists—John Paul II. Surprised? You shouldn't be. Throughout his pontificate, and especially in recent years, our Holy Father has been a "radical feminist"—radical in the sense that he attacks the "roots" of women's issues and concerns; and a feminist, speaking courageously about the irreplaceable role of women in the world and the Church and, as much as any other voice on the world stage, defending their human and civil rights.

What does the Church teach about women? Consider the following excerpts from the pope's *Letter to Women* (1995), in which he addresses important concerns about the dignity and rights of women and strongly condemns those forces in the world that oppress them:

> Women have contributed to that history [of humanity] as much as men and, more often than not, they did so in much more difficult conditions. . . . Yet how many women have been and continue to be valued more for their physical appearance than for their skill, their professionalism, their intellectual abilities, their deep sensitivity; in a word, the very dignity of their being! . . . [T]here is an urgent need to achieve *real equality* in every area: equal pay for equal work, protection for working mothers, fairness in career

advancements, equality of spouses with regard to family rights and the recognition of everything that is part of the rights and duties of citizens in a democratic State. . . . [H]ow can we not mention the long and degrading history . . . of violence against women in the area of sexuality? . . . The time has come to condemn vigorously the types of *sexual violence* which frequently have women for their object. . . . [W]hat great appreciation must be shown to those women who, with a heroic love for the child they have conceived, proceed with a pregnancy resulting from the injustice of rape . . . a crime for which guilt needs to be attributed to men and to the complicity of the general social environment (nos. 3-5, original emphasis).

And finally,

I am convinced that the secret of making speedy progress in achieving full respect for women and their identity involves more than simply the condemnation of discrimination and injustices, necessary though this may be. Such respect must first and foremost be won through an effective and intelligent *campaign for the promotion of women* (no. 6, original emphasis).

You see what I mean when I refer to the pope as a "radical feminist"? When that sad day comes that our Holy Father passes from this world to the next, women will have lost one of their staunchest and most articulate defenders.

Nor does the pope forget to extol one of the most important and beautiful contributions women make to the Church and the world, through their vocation as mothers. In one of the warmest passages of his letter, the pope writes:

Thank you, women who are mothers. . . . This experience makes you become God's own smile upon the newborn child, the one who guides your child's first steps, who helps it to grow, and who is the anchor as the child makes its way along the journey of life.

The pope calls for "an effective and intelligent campaign for the promotion of women," and there is no doubt that the world and the Church, beginning in our own backyard, have a very long way to go before women achieve full equality with men and are truly able to share their special gifts and talents.

"What about the ordination of women to the priesthood?" you ask. "If the Church is really serious about women's rights and contributions, shouldn't the priestly office be open to women?"

It is a legitimate question, and it is important that we clearly understand the teaching of the Church in that regard. It is part of our Catholic faith that "the Church has no authority whatsoever to confer priestly ordination on women." This teaching is based on the example of Christ in the Scriptures and the solemn Tradition of the Church, an unbroken 2,000-year-old practice, formed in truth by the Holy Spirit. We believe, in other words, that the practice of ordaining only men to the ministerial priesthood is in accord with God's plan for the Church, and we are not free to deviate from that plan.

Ordination to the priesthood is not a question of "rights." No one, male or female, has a "right" to be ordained. The Sacrament of Holy Orders, like all the sacraments of the Church, has been instituted by Christ and mediated and regulated by the Church, according to the will of Christ. No person has an absolute "right" to any of the sacraments.

This is a matter of faith, definitively taught by the Church. Catholics are obligated to understand and accept this teaching, as surely as we accept the teaching of the Church about the Trinity, the divinity of Christ, the Immaculate Conception, and our Blessed Mother's perpetual virginity. And like all the teachings of Christ and His Church, if we find it difficult to understand and accept, we need to be patient; we need to read, study, and pray, praying especially for the openness of heart and mind the Holy Spirit imparts.

In promoting the dignity, rights, and contributions of women, the time has come to move beyond the question of ordination to the priesthood, or we will be forever gridlocked. The question serves only as a distraction; it derails us from undertaking the "effective and intelligent campaign for the promotion of women" described by the pope. Or, in other terms, as one writer said in speaking about priestly celibacy but equally applicable here, "When we begin to concentrate on what our life isn't, and neglect to actively pursue what it is, trouble will almost certainly follow."[1]

The world and the Church should follow the example of Pope John Paul II in proclaiming and defending the dignity and equality of women. We need to do everything possible to elicit their special gifts and talents, the "genius of women," as the pope calls it. We are indeed very grateful for the gifts and talents of the dedicated and competent women who serve the Church. The Body of Christ is more complete because of their presence and service.

---

[1] Keith Clark, *An Experience of Celibacy* (Notre Dame, Ind.: Ave Maria Press, 1982), 58.

Mary: Yesterday, Today, and Tomorrow

Thus is fulfilled the prophecy of the Magnificat, "All generations will call me blessed."... Those who from generation to generation among the different peoples and nations of the earth accept with faith the mystery of Christ, the Incarnate Word and Redeemer of the world, not only turn with veneration to Mary and confidently have recourse to her as his Mother, but also seek in her faith support of their own.

These words of Pope John Paul II in his 1987 encyclical, *Redemptoris Mater* (Mother of the Redeemer), remind us that Mary shares in the eternal pilgrimage of the Church, that she has a very special place in God's work of salvation, past, present, and future. Perhaps it would be helpful to return to this beautiful document and reflect on this theme as the Church continues her pilgrimage of faith in the new millennium.

First, we turn our thoughts to the place of Mary in the history of our salvation, more particularly to those historical events by which our redemption was accomplished. Truly one cannot tell the story of Christ without reference to the story of His Mother, Mary, and conversely, the Second Vatican Council teaches us that only in the mystery of Christ can the mystery of mankind be understood. If that is true of all mankind, it is certainly true of the woman of Nazareth who became the Mother of Christ.

Mary's contribution to the drama of salvation is unique. Her singular faith and obedience to the will of God allowed God's plan to be fulfilled, and allowed Jesus to enter the world.

Mary uttered this *fiat* in faith. In faith she entrusted herself to God without reserve and "devoted herself totally as the handmaid of the Lord to the person and work of her Son" (34). And as the Fathers of the Church teach—she conceived this Son in her mind before she conceived him in her womb (no. 13).

Every aspect of Mary's life, then, was directed to and fulfilled in the life of her Son. It was Mary, better than anyone else, who understood the special nature of her Son's mission: "Do whatever he tells you" (Jn. 2:5), she instructs the servants at the wedding feast of Cana. It was Mary who stood at the foot of the Cross on Calvary, sharing the agony of her Son, representing all mankind at that moment of salvation. It was Mary who received with joy the news of the Resurrection, and it was Mary who was present in the upper room as the apostles experienced the outpouring of the Holy Spirit, that same Spirit who had touched and forever changed Mary's life at the Annunciation.

In all that she did, Mary was guided by faith. The life of Mary on earth teaches us how to accept God's will in our lives and encourages us to direct every part of our life to Jesus and in doing so have our destiny fulfilled in His.

But Mary's influence is not limited to the past, as if she were some character out of a grand historic novel. As we live in this present moment, Mary continues to be the primary model for the Church on earth:

As Virgin and Mother, Mary remains for the Church a permanent model. . . . The Church becomes herself a mother by accepting God's word with fidelity. . . . [B]y her preaching and by baptism she brings forth to a new and immortal life children who are conceived of the Holy Spirit and born of God. . . . It can be said that from Mary the Church also learns her own motherhood . . . because, receiving life from the Spirit, she "generates" sons and daughters of the human race to a new life in Christ (nos. 42-43).

If Mary is the model for the Church in her mission on earth and in her hope of future glory, she is also the role model for each individual member of the Church. Think of all the virtues Mary incorporated in her own life, and how you and I could grow in holiness—and the world with us—if we but followed her illustrious example.

In a world that attempts to live without God in its acceptance of a practical atheism, Mary reminds us that our lives have no lasting value if they are not centered on God.

In a world that is so often superficial and hurried, Mary, "who kept all these things, pondering them in her heart" (Lk. 2:19), points to the importance and power of prayer.

In a world swept up in the pursuit of material abundance, Mary, who left the comforts of her home in Nazareth to travel to Bethlehem, teaches us not to become attached to the things of this passing life.

In a world consumed by sexual gratification and addicted to carnal pleasure, Mary demonstrates the freedom of purity and the life-giving nature of virginity.

In a world that disdains the life of the unborn child, Mary, who recognized in her womb the gift of life, indeed the Lord of life, emphasizes the sanctity of human life as a precious gift of God.

And in a world that does all it can to avoid inconvenience and personal suffering, Mary, whose heart was pierced by a sword, shows us that through suffering comes strength, from death comes life.

In short, through her intercession on our behalf before the throne of Almighty God, and in her perennial example of a virtue-filled Christian life, Mary continues to bless her children in the present moment.

Mary speaks not only to the past and present, however, but also to the future blessing we expect to inherit as children of God. Mary is the sign of future glory that awaits us along with the whole Church following Mary's holy pilgrimage into heaven. As the pope has written:

> Strengthened by the presence of Christ (cf. Mt. 28:20), the Church journeys through time towards the consummation of the ages and goes to meet the Lord who comes. But on this journey—and I wish to make this point straightaway—she proceeds along the path already trodden by the Virgin Mary (no. 2).

Mary, then, honored as the Mother of the Church, leads the way for all her children as we travel through life with our hearts and souls longing for the perfection of heaven.

But what is said of the whole Church should also be said for you and me, for each and every member of the Church. Mary inspires in us the gift of hope—the virtue that lifts us from the burdensome concerns of the present moment and makes us acutely aware of our future in Christ. Hope is essential in our troubled lives, and don't we pray at every Mass that "we wait in joyful hope for the coming of our Savior, Jesus Christ"? The life and glorious victory of Mary give us hope: "In this eschatological fulfillment, Mary does not cease to be the 'Star of the Sea' (*Maris Stella*) for all those who are still on the journey of faith" (no. 6).

No event in Mary's life proclaims the virtue of hope more clearly than her glorious Assumption, body and soul, into heaven. The Church exhorts her children to pray to Mary, Queen of heaven and earth:

> Let them implore that she who aided the beginning of the Church by her prayers may now, exalted as she is in heaven above all the saints and angels, intercede with her Son in the fellowship of all the saints (no. 50).

Let us conclude as our Holy Father concluded *Redemptoris Mater*, with these words:

> As she goes forward with the whole of humanity towards the frontier between the two Millennia, the Church, for her part, with the whole community of believers and in union with all men and women of good will, takes up the great challenge contained in these words of the Marian antiphon: "the people who have fallen yet strive to rise again," and she addresses both the Redeemer and his Mother with the plea: "Assist us" (no. 52).

Illness: A Time of Crisis and Faith

[H]is disciples asked him, "Rabbi, who sinned, this man or his parents, that he was born blind?" Jesus answered, "It was not that this man sinned, or his parents, but that the works of God might be made manifest in him"

—Jn. 9:2-3

Have you ever had to deal with serious illness, either for yourself or with a family member or close friend? If so, you'd probably agree that illness can be a two-edged sword, a time of crisis and faith.

Serious illness certainly creates one of the most difficult personal crises of a lifetime. It can be a time of immense suffering and pain, a time of agonized questioning, a time when we are confronted by the prospect of our own mortality. Illness often results in a radical change in our way of life, draining all our resources—spiritual, emotional, and financial.

But good things can result from serious illness, too. Responding to the crisis of illness can bring families closer together as they rally to offer mutual support and encouragement. Illness often creates new appreciation for the little things in life, indeed for the gift of life itself. And it can be a time of renewed personal faith and spiritual growth, drawing us closer to God, leading us back to the sacraments and the community of the Church.

Within this context of suffering and salvation, the Church ministers to those who are ill and to those who provide for their care. Two recent celebrations of the Church have raised these issues. In the Youngstown Diocese we have just observed the fourth annual White Mass, at which we honor and pray for health-care professionals—doctors, nurses, administrators, chaplains, medical students, and volunteer groups.

On February 11, 2000, the Universal Church observed the eighth annual World Day for the Sick, an event that had special significance in connection with the Great Jubilee. In his annual message for this celebration, Pope John Paul II makes several points that are helpful for our reflection.

The pope reminds us, first of all, that caring for the sick was an essential part of the earthly ministry of Our Lord. How often in the Gospels we read passages such as this one:

> A great crowd . . . of people . . . came to hear him and to be healed of their diseases; . . . And all the crowd sought to touch him, for power came forth from him and healed them all (Lk. 6:17-19).

The pope invites the sick to turn to Jesus, the source of our healing and strength, "to contemplate the face of Jesus, the Divine Samaritan of souls and bodies."

In fulfilling the mission of Jesus, the Church throughout the centuries has made care of the sick one of its primary works. The pope writes:

> Sharing the joys and hopes, sorrows and anxieties of the people of every age, the Church has constantly accompanied humanity in its struggle against pain and its commitment to improve health. At the same time, she has striven to reveal to mankind the meaning of the suffering, the riches of redemption brought by Christ the Savior.

The pope explains that this "theology of suffering," expressed in illness, has meaning for all people. We believe that illness is much more than a mere expression of human frailty. It is an actual sharing in the Paschal Mystery, an opportunity for faith and spiritual growth.

We turn our gaze in particular to the suffering and risen Christ. . . . The imitation of Jesus, the Suffering Servant, has led great saints and simple believers to turn their illness and pain into a source of purification and salvation for themselves and others.

Continuing on, the pope encourages all members of the Church to embrace the sick, to care for them as a personal commitment and expression of charity:

The example of Christ, the Good Samaritan, must inspire the believer's attitude, prompting him to be close to his brothers and sisters who are suffering, through respect, understanding, acceptance, tenderness, compassion, and gratuitousness.

And finally the pope offers a special word of appreciation and encouragement to those who are involved in the health-care industry, asking them to "develop the insight of faith as they look at the sublime and mysterious value of life, even when it is frail and vulnerable." The pope challenges health care workers to be "guardians of human life."

The care of the sick—what a beautiful and important ministry this is for the Church. The sacramental expression of the Church's ministry to the sick is found, of course, in the Sacrament of the Anointing of the Sick. This sacrament is the prayer of Christ and the Church for the physical and spiritual good of a person who is seriously ill.

The scriptural basis of the sacrament is found in the ministry of Jesus Himself and more explicitly in the Letter of Saint James:

Is any among you sick? Let him call for the elders of the church, and let them pray over him, anointing him with oil in the name of the Lord; and the prayer of faith will save the sick man, and the Lord will raise him up; and if he has committed sins, he will be forgiven (Jas. 5:14-15).

The administration of the sacrament formerly known as Extreme Unction, or "the Last Rites," is today intended to include all Catholics who are seriously ill, those weakened by old age, those facing or recovering from serious surgery, the handicapped, those with mental illness, and others who are burdened by any sort of serious physical illness.

Persons who are ill may be anointed individually by a priest in the privacy of their homes or hospital room, or in a more communal setting such as a parish church, where the sick can benefit from the grace of the sacrament as well as the loving support of the Christian community. Persons who are ill should not hesitate to request the sacrament at the appropriate time. Likewise, family members of those who are ill should see to it that their loved ones receive the ministry of the Church whenever necessary.

Without a doubt, serious illness is a time of crisis. But it is also a time of faith. The passage from Saint John's Gospel quoted at the beginning of this sectoin reminds us that like the disciples wondering about the blind man, we often seek the reasons for and the meaning of illness. But as Jesus responded to His followers, so He responds to us: Moments of illness and suffering can be fruitful and redemptive, allowing the works of God to be made visible in those who believe.

Let us take this occasion to support and pray for those who care for the sick, privately and professionally. Their work is often difficult and discouraging. May the Holy Spirit direct and bless their service, which is so important for the well-being of others. May their ministry be a clear affirmation of the value and goodness of human life.

And let us also pray for all those who are ill—remembering particularly our family members and friends who are sick. May they know the healing power of Jesus, the Divine Samaritan in their lives. And by faithfully sharing in the suffering of Christ, may they come to know the fullness of the life He offers.

Pathways to Peace

Each year on January 1, the Church observes the World Day of Peace, a special time for prayer and reflection on themes related to the essential but elusive gift of peace in the world. Each year the pope sends a message to the Church and the world about peace, in which he highlights a particular theme related to the topic.

Our Holy Father's 1999 letter addresses a very comprehensive and lofty issue: the fundamental importance of human dignity and human rights. The pope's basic premise is that the true foundation of peace in the world is respect for human dignity and the promotion of the common good of society. In other words, if we respect and foster human dignity and freedom, peace will inevitably follow.

Although it is difficult to examine all the consequences of this sweeping message in a few short pages, I do wish to summarize its basic themes by sharing with you a few specific quotes from our Holy Father's letter:

• **Respect for human dignity**—"The dignity of the human person is a transcendent value, always recognized as such by those who sincerely search for the truth. Indeed, the whole of human history should be interpreted in the light of this certainty. . . . [I]t must be said again that no affront to human dignity can be ignored, whatever its source, whatever actual form it takes and wherever it occurs."

• **The universality and indivisibility of human rights**—"All human beings, without exception, are equal in dignity. For the same reason, these rights apply to every state of life and to every political, social, economic and cultural situation. . . . Defense of the universality and indivisibility of human rights is essential for the construction of a peaceful society and for the overall development of individuals, peoples and nations."

• **The right to life**—"The first of these is the basic right to life. Human life is sacred and inviolable from conception to its natural end. 'Thou shall not kill' is the divine commandment which states the limit beyond which it is never licit to go. . . . To choose life involves rejecting every form of violence: the violence of poverty and hunger, which afflicts so many human beings; the violence of armed conflict; the violence of criminal trafficking in drugs and arms; the violence of mindless damage to the natural environment."

• **Religious freedom**—"Religion expresses the deepest aspirations of the human person, shapes people's vision of the world and affects their relationships with others: basically it offers the answer to the question of the true meaning of life, both personal and communal. Religious freedom therefore constitutes the very heart of human rights."

• **The right to participate**—"All citizens have the right to participate in the life of their community: this is a conviction which is generally shared today. . . . In the context of the international community, nations and people have the right to share in the decisions which often profoundly modify their way of life."

• **The right to self-fulfillment**—"Every human person has innate abilities waiting to be developed. At stake here is the full actualization of one's own person and appropriate insertion into one's social environment. In order that this may take place, it is necessary above all to provide adequate education to those who are just beginning their lives: their future success depends on this. . . . Another fundamental right, upon which depends the attainment of a decent level of living, is the right to work."

• **Responsibility to the environment**—"The promotion of human dignity is linked to the right to a healthy environment, since this right highlights the dynamics of the relationship between the individual and society. . . . The danger of serious damage to land and sea, and to the climate, flora and fauna, calls for a profound change in modern civilization's typical consumer lifestyle, particularly in the richer countries."

• **The right to peace**—"In a sense, promoting the right to peace ensures respect for all other rights, since it encourages the building of a society in which structures of power give way to structures of cooperation, with a view to the common good. Recent history clearly shows the failure of recourse to violence as a means of resolving political and social problems. War destroys, it does not build up; it weakens the moral foundations of society and creates further divisions and long-lasting tensions."

These and other specific issues are part of the Holy Father's message for the 1999 World Day of Peace. Near the conclusion of his letter, the pope appeals to all of us to do our part:

The new millennium is close at hand, and its approach has filled the hearts of many with hope for a more just and fraternal world. . . . It is in this context that I now address you, dear Brothers and Sisters in Christ, who in all parts of the world take the Gospel as the pattern of your lives: become heralds of human dignity!

Thus at the threshold of a new millennium, the pope has placed a serious challenge before us. You and I are called to be "heralds of human dignity."

But how can we even begin to do that? The world is so large and the problems so immense. We quickly give in to discouragement, then apathy. "Can we really make any difference?" we ask ourselves. And the answer is yes, a resounding yes!

First, of course, we can pray frequently and fervently for the accomplishment of peace, justice, and human rights throughout the world. And don't discount the relevance of prayer. Prayer invokes the assistance of Almighty God, raises our awareness of the issues, and builds solidarity with our brothers and sisters everywhere.

Second, we can work in society to achieve a better and more just world. Through lobbying efforts and letter-writing campaigns, through social action and financial support, and through the electoral process. We can elect representatives who have moral vision, leaders who will enact and enforce laws and public policy that promote and defend human rights and social justice. Our participation in social action can in fact have an impact on government, nationally and locally.

And, perhaps most effectively, we can be "heralds of human dignity" in the conduct of our own daily lives. In our attitudes and actions, our words and deeds, we can strive to remove any trace of injustice, intolerance, racism, and violence—anything, in fact, that allows sins against human dignity and respect to take root and flourish. This may not change the whole world, but it does change the world around us. How often have we sung the words, "Let there be peace on earth and let it begin with me"? And it's true—peace, justice, and respect for human dignity in the world do begin with you and me, at our own doorstep.

"Tell me the weight of a snowflake," a sparrow asked a wild dove.

"Nothing more than nothing," was the answer.

"In that case, I must tell you a marvelous story," the sparrow said.

"One day I sat on a branch of a fir, close to its trunk, when it began to snow—not heavily, not in a raging blizzard—no, just like in a dream, without a sound, and without any violence. Since I had nothing better to do, I counted the snowflakes settling on the twigs and needles on my branch. Their number was exactly 3,741,952. When the 3,741,953rd snowflake dropped onto the branch—nothing more than nothing as you say—the branch broke off and fell to the ground."

And the dove responded, "Then perhaps it's true: only one person's voice is lacking for peace to come to the world."

Appendix

The Eucharist: To Be Loved, To Be Lived
A Pastoral Letter on the Centrality of the Eucharist[1]

Dear Friends in Christ:

> Jesus said to them, "Truly, truly, I say to you, unless you
> eat the flesh of the Son of man and drink his blood, you
> have no life in you; he who eats my flesh and drinks my
> blood has eternal life, and I will raise him up at the last day
> (Jn. 6:53-54).

These words of Jesus remind us as clearly as possible of the
centrality of the Eucharist to our Catholic faith. The Eucharist
is, in the simplest yet most profound of terms, the source of
life. In giving us the Eucharist at the Last Supper, Jesus gave
us His very own Body and Blood, a priceless gift, one that
enriches our spiritual lives here on earth and leads us to the
perfection of eternal life in heaven.

The Catechism teaches us again of the importance of the
Eucharist in the life of the Christian:

> The Eucharist is "the source and summit of the Christian
> life." . . . For in the blessed Eucharist is contained the whole
> spiritual good of the Church, namely Christ himself. . . .
> [B]y the Eucharistic celebration we already unite ourselves
> with the heavenly liturgy and anticipate eternal life. . . . In

---

[1] To obtain copies of Bishop Tobin's other pastoral letters—*The Sacrament of
Penance: To Receive Mercy and Favor* (March 1, 2000) and *Catholic Schools: A
Commitment Renewed* (January 7, 2001)—please write the Diocese of Youngstown,
144 W. Wood St., Youngstown, OH 44503.

brief, the Eucharist is the sum and summary of our faith (nos. 1324, 1326-27).

The teaching and lived experience of the Church have helped us to understand more fully the many dimensions of the Eucharist. It is a sacrifice—the sacrifice of Jesus on the Cross; it is a sacrament—the Real Presence of Christ under the forms of bread and wine; it is a meal—the same memorial meal Jesus shared with His apostles at the Last Supper; it is a liturgical celebration—a public proclamation of our faith in sign and symbol.

The Eucharist is all this and much more. No single one of these dimensions is sufficient unto itself to fully reveal the meaning of the Eucharist; none of them can be overlooked in fully appreciating the magnitude of the gift. The Eucharist is an inexhaustible mystery: to be loved, to be lived.

Our shared preparation for the coming of the third millennium also centers on and leads us to the Eucharist. As the Holy Father writes in *Tertio Millennio Adveniente*:

[S]ince Christ is the only way to the Father . . . [t]he year 2000 will be intensely Eucharistic: in the *Sacrament of the Eucharist* the Savior, who took flesh in Mary's womb twenty centuries ago, continues to offer himself to humanity as the source of divine life (no. 55).

Certainly every active member of the Church recognizes and fully appreciates the centrality of the Eucharist in our individual Catholic lives and in the communal life of the Church. No person of authentic Catholic faith will deny the teaching of the Church about the Eucharist.

And yet, because of human nature, we often take our gifts for granted, even the most special of our gifts—our life, our health, our family, our friends, and our faith. It is even possible, because of our weakness and perhaps because the Eucharist is so readily available to us, to take the

Eucharist for granted and to become less than clear about its meaning and importance.

Recent surveys throughout the nation have suggested that this is exactly what has taken place in the Church. And while the validity and meaning of the surveys can be questioned, they do raise serious concerns and challenge us to renew our understanding and appreciation of the most Blessed Sacrament.

For some time now, in a number of different settings, I have been discussing questions related to the Eucharist. This topic has been presented at meetings of the Priests' Council, the Pastoral Council, and priests within their deaneries. I have discussed it formally and informally. These discussions have been extremely valuable and a number of important insights and suggestions have been shared.

It is encouraging to note, first of all, that the Church in Youngstown does truly understand the teaching of the Church about the Eucharist and appreciates it as the foundation of our spiritual life, the "sum and summary of our faith." There is also a general consensus that most Catholics have a ready understanding of the Catholic teaching about the Real Presence of Christ in the Eucharist, that

> [i]n the most blessed sacrament of the Eucharist "the body and blood, together with the soul and divinity, of our Lord Jesus Christ and, therefore, *the whole Christ is truly, really, and substantially* contained" (Catechism, no. 1374, original emphasis).

The conversations I have had concerning the Eucharist are, therefore, most encouraging. And I might add that my own travels through the diocese and my participation in the liturgies of our parishes have confirmed that estimation.

At the same time, however, most of our recent discussions have also suggested that we need constantly to affirm the teaching of the Church about the Eucharist, that it is necessary to stress, again and again, the profound meaning of the Eucharist so that we never lose sight of its beauty and importance. Some have suggested that, in particular, younger Catholics may not have received clear, sufficient teaching about the Eucharist and that we have a special obligation to reach out to them with this message.

During our discussions I regularly asked what the Church in the Diocese of Youngstown might do to strengthen our understanding of the teaching about the Eucharist. In response, a number of very practical, specific suggestions were offered. I offer them to you here with the hope that they will provide a starting point for additional and prayerful reflection:

(1) The key to maintaining our belief in the Real Presence of Christ in the Eucharist is the faithful and vibrant celebration of the Sunday Eucharist.

As Roger Cardinal Mahony, Archbishop of Los Angeles, wrote in his recent pastoral letter about Sunday Mass:

> We the Church assemble on the Lord's Day, and that assembly, in the name of the Father and the Son and the Holy Spirit, speaks and listens to the Word of God, makes holy and is made holy by its Eucharistic praying and the sacred banquet of Holy Communion.[2]

Cardinal Mahony's words echo those of the Catechism:

> It was above all on "the first day of the week," Sunday, the day of Jesus' resurrection, that the Christians met "to break bread." From that time on down to our day the celebration of the Eucharist has been continued so that today we encounter it everywhere in the Church with the same fundamental structure. It remains the center of the Church's life (no. 1343).

---

[2] *Gather Faithfully Together: A Guide for Sunday Mass.*

I invite the parishes of the Youngstown diocese to review their celebration of the Sunday Eucharist to ensure that it is both faithful and vibrant: faithful to the liturgical directives of the Church and vibrant in encouraging all of God's People toward the "full, conscious, and active participation" demanded by the very nature of the liturgy. And parishes should continue to reach out to those members who do not regularly attend Sunday Mass, inviting them to become a part of the Eucharistic community.

In highlighting the centrality of Sunday Eucharist, we should not overlook the wonderful tradition of daily Mass, which is expected of our priests, and which many of the faithful find to be a source of great comfort and blessing in their lives.

(2) Pastors and catechists should use special moments throughout the liturgical year to teach the people, especially young people, about the Real Presence of Christ in the Eucharist.

The liturgical year of the Church provides frequent opportunities to speak about the Eucharist. Such occasions would include the celebration of First Holy Communion in the parish, the Solemnities of Corpus Christi and Christ the King, Holy Thursday, the Easter season, and other occasions when the Scriptures lend themselves to Eucharistic themes.

We should be especially attentive to children and young people to be certain that in the formative years of their lives, they are receiving clear and direct teaching about the Catholic understanding of the Eucharist.

Our teaching about the Eucharist should be a constant, ongoing process so that the People of God are frequently reminded of the beauty of the holy mystery in their midst.

(3) Parishes and institutions should carefully review how the Blessed Sacrament is handled.

In some of our discussions, the point was made that the manner in which we handle the Eucharist is a powerful sign of what we believe about the Eucharist. It was also suggested that familiarity may breed carelessness with the Eucharist.

Questions to be considered: Do we carry, receive, distribute, and reserve the Eucharist with obvious reverence? Do we remember that "[t]he Eucharistic presence of Christ begins at the moment of consecration and endures as long as the Eucharistic species subsist" (Catechism, no. 1377)? Are we careful and prayerful as we purify the sacred vessels after Mass, knowing that they continue to contain the Body and Blood of the Lord? Is our use of language consistent with what we believe about the Eucharist: Do we speak merely about "bread and wine," or do we refer to the elements as the "Body and Blood of Christ" they have truly become?

While it is not necessary to return to the scrupulosity that may have characterized some in the past, neither should we succumb to a secular, materialistic, and casual approach to the Eucharist sometimes evident today.

(4) In churches where the Blessed Sacrament is reserved in a separate chapel, there should be a concerted effort to remind the faithful of that fact and to promote attention to the reserved Eucharist.

Liturgical law allows for the placement of the Blessed Sacrament in separate chapels in our churches, but the purpose of that reservation is surely not to distance the Eucharist from the people, but to encourage prayerful, distraction-free adoration of the Lord Jesus. As the Catechism reminds us:

The *tabernacle* is to be situated "in churches in a most worthy place with the greatest honor." The dignity, placing, and security of the Eucharistic tabernacle should foster adoration before the Lord really present in the Blessed Sacrament of the altar (no. 1183, original emphasis).

Additionally, the Code of Canon Law states: "The tabernacle in which the most Holy Eucharist is reserved is to be situated in some part of the church or oratory which is distinguished, conspicuous, beautifully decorated, and suitable for prayer" (canon 938).

The place where the Blessed Sacrament is reserved should be very evident to the faithful, and "[a] special lamp which indicates and honors the presence of Christ is to shine continuously before a tabernacle in which the Most Holy Eucharist is reserved" (canon 940).

The traditional Catholic practice of genuflecting upon entering and leaving the Church, and when passing in front of the Blessed Sacrament, should be maintained, as an external sign of our awareness of and respect for Christ's presence.

(5) Parishes should seriously consider the reestablishment of traditional practices that foster devotion to the presence of Christ in the Blessed Sacrament.

As noted earlier, the celebration of the Sunday Eucharist is clearly the center of the Church's life. At the same time, the Sunday Eucharist does not exhaust the prayer of the Church related to the Eucharist:

> The Catholic Church has always offered and still offers to the sacrament of the Eucharist the cult of adoration, not only during Mass, but also outside of it, reserving the consecrated hosts with the utmost care, exposing them to the solemn veneration of the faithful, and carrying them in procession (Catechism, no. 1378).

I commend the parishes of the diocese that have maintained the beautiful practice of Forty Hours or Eucharistic days, and other regular periods of adoration, and I invite other parishes to initiate these celebrations as well.

> In churches where the Eucharist is reserved, it is recommended that solemn exposition of the Blessed Sacrament for an extended period of time should take place once a year. . . . In this way, the local community may meditate on this mystery more deeply and adore.[3]

Such devotions will also provide a fitting preparation for the coming of the third millennium which, as our Holy Father reminds us, is meant to be "intensely Eucharistic."

Some parishes of the diocese have received permission for perpetual exposition of the Eucharist. The Church does not envision this becoming a widespread practice. However, where it has begun, perpetual adoration has been a source of many blessings and graces. I commend the priests, deacons, religious, and faithful who devote themselves to this discipline.

Some have maintained that promoting adoration of the Blessed Sacrament will take away from the centrality of the Eucharistic celebration. It need not do so. In fact, proper devotion to the Blessed Sacrament will inevitably lead to a fuller participation in the Eucharistic celebration:

> Outside the Eucharistic celebration, the Church is careful to venerate the Blessed Sacrament, which must be reserved . . . as the spiritual center of the religious and parish community. Contemplation prolongs Communion and enables one to meet Christ, true God and true man, in a lasting way. . . .

---

[3] Sacred Congregation for Divine Worship, Decree on Holy Communion and Worship of the Eucharist outside Mass *Eucharistiae Sacramentum* (June 21, 1973), no. 86.

[P]rayer of adoration in the presence of the Blessed Sacrament unites the faithful with the paschal mystery; it enables them to share in Christ's sacrifice, of which the Eucharist is the permanent sacrament.[4]

Others have suggested that the adoration of the Blessed Sacrament causes people to withdraw from the cares and concerns of the world. But in fact, as the Holy Father writes:

Closeness to Christ in silence and contemplation does not distance us from our contemporaries, but, on the contrary, makes us attentive and open to human joy and distress and broadens our heart on a global scale.[5]

In recent times, the beautiful example of Mother Teresa of Calcutta, who every day spent considerable time with the Blessed Sacrament before serving the "poorest of the poor," helps to illustrate the Holy Father's observation.

This dimension of the Eucharist is highlighted at the conclusion of every Mass with the words "Go in peace to love and serve the Lord." Indeed, through our lives of faithful and generous service, the meaning of the Eucharist is completely revealed.

In short, the liturgical celebration of the Eucharist, the reception of Holy Communion, the adoration of the Blessed Sacrament, and our commitment to service need not and should not be exclusive of one another. In fact, these practices, taken together, help us to experience the fullness of the presence of Christ in the Eucharist and motivate us to carry Christ to the world.

It should be obvious that this letter does not intend to present the full teaching of the Church about the Eucharist or

---

[4] Pope John Paul II, Letter on the 750th Anniversary of the Feast of Corpus Christi (May 28, 1996), no. 3.
[5] Ibid.

its profound meaning in our lives. Nor does it attempt a full discussion of the themes contained therein.

The suggestions outlined in this letter were offered during the conversations about the Eucharist which took place in the Diocese of Youngstown, and I am grateful for all those who shared in these discussions with such obvious faith, insight, and candor.

In my view, the most important thing is that the conversations about the Eucharist continue. And it is in our parishes that the teaching of the Church is best presented and devotion to the Real Presence of Christ best preserved.

Therefore, I ask that in every parish of the diocese these themes be discussed from the pulpit and in the classrooms, in meetings of the parish councils and parish organizations. I request that this letter be the starting point of the conversation, but you may wish to provide other material as well. I call your attention especially to the *Catechism of the Catholic Church* and its treatment of the Eucharist in nos. 1322-1419.

I believe that the Eucharistic faith of the Church in the Diocese of Youngstown is strong and clear, and for that we give thanks to Almighty God. May our anticipation of the third millennium, and our observance of this Lenten and Easter season, allow us to be a truly Eucharistic people, a people that celebrates the Mass faithfully, receives the Lord worthily, adores His presence unceasingly, and lives the Eucharist in a "life poured out in loving service of the kingdom" (Opening Prayer for the Solemnity of Corpus Christi).

Sincerely yours in Christ, Our Lord,
Most Rev. Thomas J. Tobin
Bishop of Youngstown
February 25, 1998